Lecture Notes of the Institute for Computer Sciences, Social-Informatics and Telecommunications Engineering 38

Adolfo Villafiorita Regis Saint-Paul
Alessandro Zorer (Eds.)

E-Infrastructures and E-Services on Developing Countries

First International ICST Conference, AFRICOMM 2009
Maputo, Mozambique, December 3-4, 2009
Proceedings

Springer

Volume Editors

Adolfo Villafiorita
Fondazione Bruno Kessler
via Sommarive 18
38100 Trento, Italy
E-mail: adolfo.villafiorita@fbk.eu

Regis Saint-Paul
CREATE-NET
via alla Cascata 56/D
38123 Trento, Italy
E-mail: regis.saint-paul@create-net.org

Alessandro Zorer
CREATE-NET
via alla Cascata 56/D
38123 Trento, Italy
E-mail: alessandro.zorer@create-net.org

Library of Congress Control Number: 2010925233

CR Subject Classification (1998): C.2, H.4, D.2, H.3, H.5, F.2

ISSN	1867-8211
ISBN-10	3-642-12700-2 Springer Berlin Heidelberg New York
ISBN-13	978-3-642-12700-7 Springer Berlin Heidelberg New York

springer.com

Printed in Germany

Typesetting: Camera-ready by author, data conversion by Scientific Publishing Services, Chennai, India
Printed on acid-free paper SPIN: 06/3180 5 4 3 2 1 0

Preface

The first edition of a conference is a significant organizational and scientific gamble. In some cases, these challenges are rewarded by results well above the initial expectations. AFRICOMM 2009, the First International ICST Conference on e-Infrastructure and e-Services for Developing Countries, was clearly one of such cases.

The conference aimed at bringing together international researchers, public officers, policy makers and practitioners in ICT to discuss issues and trends, recent research, innovation advances, and on-the-field experiences related to e-Government, e-Governance, e-Infrastructure, and e-Business, with a focus on developing countries. It is in fact widely accepted that ICT Infrastructure and (e-*)services are key drivers for development, well-being, and improved quality of life. This was also highlighted by Kofi Annan, former UN General Secretary, in 2002: "While ICT cannot address all of [Africa's] problems, they can do much to place Africa on a firmer industrial footing... and strengthen the continent's human resources, with training that leads to sustainable livelihoods."

AFRICOMM 2009 was organized in three tracks: two of them organized as Research Tracks, on Information and Communication Infrastructures and on e-Services for Developing Countries, and one Policy and Governance Track. Contributions to the first two tracks were selected by peer-review, while the policies session involved key stakeholders in the areas of ICT, development, and policy making who submitted position papers. Participation and selection of papers for the tracks was quite good. In total, 32 paper were submitted, 17 of which for the e-Services track and 15 for the e-Infrastructure track. Of these, 17 were selected and included in the final program.

Concerning the e-Services track, on top of areas, such as e-Learning and e-Health, which traditionally have played a major role in fostering development, the conference highlighted the increasing importance of e-Government services. Mobile technologies represent in Africa (as well as in the rest of the world) the most promising means to narrow the digital divide and provide services to citizens located also in rural areas. This was highlighted by virtually all experiences presented at the conference. We expect this trend to continue in the coming years.

During the discussion on the ICT infrastructures dedicated to fostering technologies and projects in and for developing countries, key technical trends were highlighted, focusing on the challenges and on real-world deployments. A recurring theme on the challenges side was on how to provide ICT infrastructures in rural areas and how to combine different technologies that provide better value for emerging regions. Some of the technologies, such as mobile and wireless mesh networks were also discussed in depth as low-cost solutions to cover the vaster regions with basic infrastructures. Very relevant user cases were presented and we expect many others will follow the same trends in the future.

The Policy and Governance Track was organized as high-level round tables among the following themes: ICTs in the policy cycle—innovating policy making by mainstreaming ICTs into the current policy agenda; public administration and public investment priorities—ICTs and basic service delivery for marginalized populations; and mobile technologies and development policies—reaching the unreached on a sustainable basis. All of them were stimulating positive and fruitful discussions among the speakers and between them and the conference attendees. Some of the good examples of real-world deployment and services presented during the research tracks were discussed here in terms of the public policies to make these few cases the driver for a larger impact on the region and to make sustainable in the long term the initial investments that have been made.

Having appreciated some many positive interactions on the discussion between the infrastructure and the services communities and between them and the policy makers, confirmed the strong value of the initial idea of establishing a new forum for discussing ICT challenges and trends on developing countries with a target making a positive impact on regions, citizens, businesses, and governments in those areas.

Organization

Steering Committee

Imrich Chlamtac (Chair)	CREATE-NET, Italy
Salomao Julio Manhica	UTICT, Mozambique
Fausto Giunchiglia	University of Trento, Italy
Paolo Traverso	FBK, Center for Information Technology, Italy

Conference General Chair

Radu Popescu Zeletin — Fraunhofer FOKUS, Germany

Conference General Vice Chair

Alessandro Zorer — CREATE-NET, Italy

Technical Program Chair

Lourino Chemane — UTICT, Mozambique

Technical Program Vice Chair

Darelle van Greunen — N. Mandela Metropolitan University, South Africa

e-Infrastructure Track Chair

Karl Jonas — Fraunhofer FOKUS, Germany

e-Services Track Chair

Adolfo Villafiorita — FBK Center for Information Technology, Italy

e-Policy Track Chair

Raul Zambrano — UNDP, USA

Workshop Chair

Segopotso Moshapo	SAP Research, South Africa

Local Chair

Augusto Nunes	UTICT, Mozambique

Conference Coordinator

Maria Morozova	Institute for Computer Sciences, Social Informatics and Telecommunications Engineering (ICST)

Technical Program Committee

Lasse Berntzen	Vestfold University College, Norway
Love Ekenberg	Stockholm University, Sweden
Stephen Flowerday	University of Fort Hare, South Africa
Marlien Herselman	CSIR Meraka Institute, South Africa
Robert Krimmer	E-Voting.CC, Austria
Jude Lubega	Makerere University, Uganda
Esselina Macome	Eduardo Mondlane University, Mozambique
Mohamed Mosbah	Université Bordeaux, France
Americo Muchanga	Eduardo Mondlane University, Mozambique
Regis Saint-Paul	CREATE-NET, Italy
Efthimios Tambouris	University of Macedonia, Greece
Oliver Popov	Stockholm University, Sweden
Idris Rai	Makarere University, Uganda
Pavel Shvaiko	Informatica Trentina, Italy
Komminist Weldemariam	FBK Center for Information Technology, Italy
Raffaele De Amicis	Graphitech, Italy
Bartel Van de Walle	Tilburg University, The Netherlands
Guy Weets	University of Luxembourg, Luxembourg
Christopher G. Reddick	The University of Texas at San Antonio, USA
Anthony Ming	The Commonwealth Secretariat, UK
Thomas Magedanz	Technical University Berlin, Germany
Christoph Meinel	Hasso-Plattner-Institut / SAP, Germany
Dirk Elias	Fraunhofer Portugal Research, Portugal
Dimitrios Serpanos	University of Patras, Greece
Yuji Inoue	Telecommunication Technology Committee, Japan
Ahmed N. Tantawy	IBM Middle East & North Africa, Egypt
Christoph Schetelich	Detecon International GmbH, South Africa
Adel Al-Hezmi	Saudi Telecom Company, Saudi Arabia
Muhammad Sher	International Islamic University Islamabad, Pakistan

Gerard Le Lann	INRIA, France
Farouk Kamoun	University of Manouba, Tunisia
Juha Zidbeck	VTT, Finland
Nicolas Chevrollier	TNO ICT, The Netherlands
Dirk Hetzer	TDF/Media-Broadcast, Germany
Gertjan van Stam	Linknet, Zambia
Fiona Williams	Ericsson, Germany
Serge Fdida	University Pierre et Marie Curie-LIP6/CNRS, France

Table of Contents

Fostering Learning through the Use of Argumentative Serious Games

Markos Hatzitaskos and Nikos Karacapilidis

IMIS Lab, MEAD, University of Patras, 26500 Rio Patras, Greece
mhatzitaskos@gmail.com,
nikos@mech.upatras.gr

Abstract. As broadly admitted in the related literature, argumentation can promote learning, teamwork and leadership skills. These skills are central to the future of both developed and developing countries; however, related work reveals that students have difficulties in creating logical arguments. Motivated by the above, this paper proposes an innovative learning technology that aims at supporting argumentation through the use of serious games. Serious games have been shown to engage and motivate users and can be built with limited resources in mind. We comment on the suitability of their features for argumentation purposes, and we discuss how their use on teaching argumentation can be beneficial.

Keywords: e-Learning, Argumentation, Serious Games, ICT, Edutainment.

1 Introduction

Argumentation, i.e., the coordination of evidence and theory to support or refute an explanatory conclusion, model or prediction, has been recognized as a critically important epistemic task and discourse process. It plays a central role to learning, in which students develop explanations and argue. Admittedly, argumentation develops knowledge and provides a rich environment for students to learn effective leadership and teamwork skills [1]. These skills are beneficial to fostering the development of countries, since students will be able to work more efficiently and as a team for the betterment of their counties in the future.

Students, however, show difficulties in creating logical and reasoned arguments. The related literature (e.g. [2]) calls attention to the fact that students may increase their learning when they are actively - rather than passively - acquiring new knowledge. In order to enable students to actively acquire new knowledge, just triggering argumentation is not enough; it is important to create environments in which meaningful arguments are rewarding.

Related research reveals that even when instructing students to ask questions, although the quantity of the argumentation increased, the quality did not. For instance, as discussed in [3] after conducting a series of studies in an educational setting, although students seemed able to engage in argumentation, they only did

A. Villafiorita, R. Saint-Paul, and A. Zorer (Eds.): AFRICOMM 2009, LNICST 38, pp. 1–10, 2010.

so in situations that served some useful goal. In other words, students engaged in argumentation only when they were motivated.

The approach taken by instructors in traditional classroom activities inhibits the social discourse of critically attending to, defending and evaluating understandings. These activities are largely characterized by the instructor asking a question, students answering and the instructor responding, preventing the students from arguing their positions with fellow students or the instructor. This teaching style does not promote the idea that students should understand each other's ideas and build upon each other's knowledge. Motivating and enabling students to do so is crucial to fostering argumentation [4].

Generally speaking, argumentation has two basic constituents, namely the sense making and the discourse. Both of these aspects constitute problems to students, as they may not be able to distinguish between theories and evidence that supports them, and may confuse evidence with coherence or plausibility [5]. For this aspect of argumentation to be tamed, students should be aided in order to distinguish and value evidence from theories.

As results from the above, in order to foster learning through the use of argumentation, we need to motivate and enable students to engage in student-to-student discussions through well-prescribed activities. In this paper, we propose the development and use of a serious game to explicitly cater for teaching argumentation. We believe that well-developed and properly used serious games can augment students' motivation, by immersing them in a situation that they find engaging, as well as guide them through the understanding of different ideas and the difference between theories and evidence. Furthermore, the serious game proposed can provide a unique environment for students to take up leadership roles and improve their teamwork skills, since, in the virtual wold, they can have official authority as well as be hold accountable, by other students, if not performing as agreed [6].

2 Related Work

As stated above, students show difficulties when engaging in argumentation as they construct discussions and/or produce arguments that are not targeted or meaningful. In most cases, no counterarguments are given in such discussions. Furthermore, students produce arguments through which no conflicts arise and, as such, they are not constructive since the argumentation cannot continue. This leads to students not nurturing their argumentation, teamwork and leadership roles that would otherwise help them in real-life situations and at improving their society as a whole.

Related work has shown that practical aspects of research in the field of argumentation in education seem to be undermined by the fact that situations that favor debates, argumentation and learning within a suitable topic are not present (e.g. [1], [4]). Researchers have identified that fostering motivation in students to attend to each other's ideas is of crucial importance to the outcome of the argumentation and knowledge building [3], [4].

More specifically, Veerman and her colleagues have focused on discovering principles for the design of educational tasks that provoke collaborative argumentation [3]. Their approach includes studies of groups of students working with and without instructors and computer-supported systems, being told to engage in argumentation. They conclude that each educational situation has specific needs that must be addressed to promote argumentation. More recent approaches concentrate on creating activities that motivate students to take into account each other's ideas and support the alignment between claims and evidence [1], [4] .

Gorlinsky et al [6] have taken Veerman's work one step further and research how to leverage online games for teaching student leadership and teamwork. They concentrate on business college classrooms of developed countries, where Internet and computer access is widely available, and thus propose a solution that has a relatively high cost of implementation. However, their research is very useful since it can aid the development of a low cost serious game for developing countries that will offer a similar experience to high cost serious games and also promote teamwork and leadership.

An alternative teaching method supporting argumentation is known as 'concept cartoons' [7]. In this method, alternative ideas regarding a scientific phenomenon are presented in a form of cartoon-style drawing in a poster. Thus, ideas are put forward by cartoon characters in a discussion format and the learners are invited to join the debate with the cartoon character. The criteria for concept cartoons is to focus on probable situations rather than theory, use minimal amounts of text, and promote every alternative as of equal status. Research findings show that this approach is effective with learners of all ages and backgrounds, as it provides an intriguing new perspective on familiar events. Furthermore, it can be used in both formal and informal everyday settings. However, the concept cartoons teaching method has two significant drawbacks. Firstly, the depth of the topics discussed is limited because of the minimal text on the posters, and secondly, the strategy's purpose is only to engage interest and provoke thoughtfulness. It is not used to actually present information on a topic.

Our approach to fostering learning builds upon the integration of the abovementioned studies with the features of serious games. We argue that this alternative approach will provide students with the missing motivation that other approaches did not yield and at a low cost. Serious games will engage students and make them interested in the outcome of argumentations on various subjects between fellow students. On the other hand, instructors will not need to push students to defend their positions or ask them to engage in argumentation, since students will be motivated to do so on their own. Contrary to the concept cartoons approach discussed above, our approach will support various informational levels on a topic and as such it could be used to present a topic thoroughly. The information provided for a topic would start simple as in the concept cartoons approach, but the learner would be able to go deeper into the subject that she is interested in.

3 Serious Games

Serious games is a general term, whose precise definition seems to vary depending on the area of practice in which they are applied. However, most would agree upon the definition that serious games are games used for purposes other than mere entertainment [8] They are not a new genre per se, but rather a new perspective into how the use of games can be used for the betterment of education. Although serious games can take many forms, in this paper we are interested in serious games through the use of ICT.

The main reason we argue that the use of serious games can foster learning is the immersion and engagement they attain and sustain from the users [9]. Successful serious games provide a unique learning experience that aid recall and information retrieval. Strategic skills, analytical skills and insight for a task can also be acquired by the use of serious games [10]. Furthermore, multiplayer technology in on-line community games also fosters the creation of collaborative knowledge and develops information-seeking habits [11]. The nature of the learning supported by games has been divided into three types: (i) learning as a result of tasks stimulated by the content of the games, (ii) knowledge developed through the content of the game, and (iii) skills arising as a result of playing the game [12]. Argumentation, leadership and teamwork can all be fostered though all three types as long as they are correctly supported by the game.

Although serious games are an effective way of learning, not all games are good for all learners and for all learning outcomes. That is why to date there are serious games that deal explicitly with various subjects, such as health, social issues, politics, etc. (see http://www.seriousgames.org/). There have been numerous examples where serious games have been successfully developed and used to improve learning (e.g. [13], [14]).

3.1 Argumentative Serious Games

Our approach on fostering learning is through the use of argumentative serious games. To the best of our knowledge, there has been no serious game developed or used so far to promote argumentation explicitly. In this subsection, we attempt to justify the reasons that support our approach. That is, why combining argumentation with serious games is coherent, meaningful and promising. To do that, we investigate the features of argumentation and how they can be effectively aligned with those of serious games to provide a richer learning approach.

Argumentation takes place between a proposition and a critic. One group puts an idea forward with supporting evidence, while another group tries to refute it with contradicting evidence to support a different idea. As such, a core feature of argumentation is its inherent competition between the proposition and the critic. Games, on their whole, are played between players that compete to win, much like the proposition and the critic. As serious games are games, they can support and enhance competition through the use of various techniques such as competitive scoring. This approach to competition can be accomplished in a way that will promote fun and augment motivation for argumentation between the involved parties.

As previously stated, the proposition and the critic both support certain ideas, which they try to defend and justify. Thus, the proposition and the critic play different roles, approach an idea through different perspectives, and interact to reach a certain conclusion. Games, in general, require players to take up different roles and interact by role-playing. Serious games can well support these features of argumentation, by providing an interactive and role-playing environment. These features can be supported either in single player mode, where the computer can play the other roles, or in multiplayer mode, where human players interact. Multiplayer support also addresses the connectiveness between the subjects that argue since argumentation is a social activity (a rational activity between groups of individuals and ideas, which are connected).

Arguments are structured and their components can be modeled [15]. All arguments have a claim, some evidence and reasoning to connect the two. Some arguments are harder to follow than others and the ability to differentiate between claims, evidence and reasoning is crucial to both creating a valid argument and understanding one. The learning approach to this structure and the components can be accomplished in a fun and intuitive way through the use of serious games. Furthermore, different ability levels in argumentation can be effectively approached by the use of different difficulty levels in serious games.

In order to learn through argumentation, one has to have a grasp of understanding and identifying arguments and the goals of the participants, as well as identifying the premises from which conclusions are derived. Serious games can be used to promote learning through the acquiring of analytical, strategic skills and insight, in an amusing and intuitive way that engages players and increases replayability.

Three more characteristics that align perfectly in both argumentation and serious games are the following [6]. Both in argumentation and serious games individuals have to make quick decisions with incomplete information and be able to change course when it is necessary. Furthermore, serious games encourages students to take risks, even in the face of likely failure and at the same time risk-taking is inherit in argumentation as the proposition tries to persuade the critic to embrace an idea. Finally, both serious games and argumentation teach to plan first and act second. As is true in real life, individuals and teams may initially decide to approach a problem with an *ad hoc* way. However, they soon realize that failing occurs more often than succeeding and that thinking and planning a strategy beforehand will often save time and improve their chances of success.

3.2 Educational and COTS Serious Games

There are two kinds of serious games that can be used for our purposes. The first one concerns explicitly designed and implemented games that aim to be used mainly in a learning environment, whereas the second one concerns commercial off-the-shelf (COTS) games, designed for the entertainment market, that are filtered to provide the learning required. Both kinds have arguments for and against them, which we discuss in this section, and also require instructor support as to how to be used in teaching [16].

Educational games: Educational games are designed and implemented explicitly to promote a learning outcome. They are built in accordance with pedagogical theories and may provide additional educational information as to how they may be used in a classroom or otherwise. Being games, they are build to provide the user with the correct amount of balance between fun and learning. Furthermore, they can be developed in such a way so as to address real-world problems, either explicitly or implicitly, and present how the skills learned can be used in real-world examples. This fact is crucial as students often complain that they see few real-world applications for what they learn [17].

As far as the development of educational games is concerned, it can be an expensive process, although there has been evidence that low-budget, with mediocre graphics, but well designed games have been used successfully to promote a learning outcome [13]. In our case, the most crucial issue when committed to this kind of games is to assure the proper integration of argumentation and pedagogical features.

COTS games: As argued in [8], a games purpose may be formulated by the user herself or by the game's designer, which means that COTS games, used for non-entertainment purposes, may be also considered as serious games as long as they are used in such a way. Using COTS as serious games has the benefit that there are minimal development costs. Successful COTS games encompass fun and have a high degree of engagement, which reduces the risks of creating a game with no such elements. The designer needs to think of ways to promote a particular learning outcome by creating learning activities or modifying the game in such a way so as to support the learning required. Integration of the appropriate argumentation features should comply with the above. On the down side, instructors must put a lot of effort into creating a lesson plan using COTS games. Information in games can range from fictitious to factual and can also present principles in a haphazard and disorganized fashion. Moreover, there may exist biases and preconditions that underlie these games. The instructor needs to discover and take all these facts into account.

3.3 Serious Game Features

Apart from deciding on whether to develop or use an existing game for our purposes, it is wise to look into what features the game should have. A core feature is stealth learning. Stealth learning can be defined as when the learners are so caught up in their goals that they do not realize they are learning [18]. To do so, it is crucial to disconnect the object of the game from the instructor's assessment mechanism. That is, the student should learn the necessary information in an implicit manner rather than just for an exam.

A 2008 TEEM report [12] produced a list of features that should be supported by serious games. Clear objectives and goals, tracking of player progression levels, restarting from a save point, catering for different ability levels of users and interactiveness were some of the features identified, which are also crucial in our case. Students in game progression should also be recorded to cater for instructor needs.

As far as the complexity of the proposed type of games is concerned, there are a number of variables to consider. Complex games, being more challenging in general, offer more potential for in-classroom activities. However, complex games tend to be time-consuming, whereas technically sophisticated games are difficult to incorporate in short lesson times [16].

Prensky [19] states that a feature approach to developing a serious game is flawed, because although these elements are indeed found in good games, just encompassing the list does not guarantee a good game. He suggests at looking into games that work and try to capture their style of putting these elements together. As such, a list of features is crucial, but should not be the only guideline to design. Thus, successful working examples, based on well-tried argumentation models and mechanisms, should also be studied and taken into account.

Serious games to address issues closely related to argumentation, such as decision making and collaboration, have been already developed. At the same time, various initiatives have been formed to promote serious games for particular sectors [20]. There is an ongoing list of serious games that deal with an ever increasing variety of issues. A list of serious games used for a number of learning outcomes can be found in [14].

4 Use of Serious Games in Formal Educational Settings

Several projects have been conducted aiming to understand the implications and potential use of serious games in formal education, so as to provide a strategy for future educational development requirements (e.g. [12], [21]). This strategy, as far as this paper is concerned, is the same for both developed and developing countries. The only difference lies in the designing and implementation of serious games for different available resources. Both students and instructors have reported that the use of games in lessons was motivating. Furthermore, the above-mentioned reports highlighted the numerous strengths that games have, including their ability to promote collaboration, foster engagement and develop students' thinking and skills, including leadership skills.

However, there were also some practical difficulties that needed to be addressed, such as the fact that the fixed length of most learning sessions was constraining in both the planning and the implementation of game-based learning. Moreover, the reports indicated that although instructors need a certain level of familiarity with the game used in their teaching, achieving educational and learning objectives through the game was more dependent on the instructor's knowledge of the curriculum to be taught, as well as other abilities related to teaching. The proposed integration of argumentation features has the potential to facilitate both instructors and students.

As serious games are entering the world of education and training, the role of the instructors will shift. Instructors will be faced with a changing profession and will need to be educated on how to teach using this new technology. In developing countries this poses a further problem as qualified instructors in formal education are exiguous and their training on how to teach using this new technology will be scarce. This problem is probably greater than the fact that there are very few physical resources where to deploy serious games. That is, even if there are enough computers to use in the classroom, if the instructor does not know how to incorporate and use the serious games available in his curriculum efficiently, the desired effect will not be achieved. As such, a solution proposed especially for serious games developed for developing countries is to design and implement games that would be intuitive for the instructor to learn, that would have clear goals so as to help the instructor to incorporate them in his class, as well as be low-budget and require low computing resources. Furthermore, serious games for developing countries should take into account the fact that there may be only one computer in every classroom.

The role that does stay the same for the instructor is the role of motivator (understanding students and their needs, and steering them in the most engaging direction). Style, passion and presentation abilities still remain key roles for instructors. Instructors however, as stated in [14], have to take the role of content structurer, as well as that of integrator and reformulator. This is because content, for serious games, must be presented in a very different approach (compared to traditional ones) to be effective. Furthermore, another role for instructors using serious games is that of the debriefer. As a debriefer, the instructor helps students reflect on what is being learned. This is necessary because even if serious games motivated students enough to go through the material, it would not always be clear that the conclusions they drew, as well as the mental models and ideas they learned, were the ones intended; moreover, whether they would be able to apply what they learned in future situations [14].

Creating an argumentative serious game to foster learning in formal educational settings should take into account the abovementioned issues and provide proper solutions for the diverse and complementary roles of the instructor. It should be an easy to use game, designed to be used within specific time limits. In addition, it should be helpful to the instructor in her work towards motivating students to engage in argumentation. This game should present the content to be learned under a different lens, where the instructor could potentially be an integral part of the game by encapsulating an in-game role and interactively playing the role of the motivator, content structurer and debriefer.

5 Conclusion and Future Work

In this paper, we have argued that using serious games can be an effective alternative approach to promote argumentation and foster learning, as well as nurture various other skills, such as teamwork and leadership. These skills can be of great assistance to the future of developing countries, as students who are taught argumentation, teamwork and leadership correctly, will be able to work more efficiently and as a team for the betterment of their countries.

We looked into the importance of argumentation, as well as the current inability of students in creating logical and reasoned arguments. We also reviewed related literature on teaching argumentation and identified the lack of motivation that students have in attending to each other's ideas. We presented serious games, their benefits and how they could be used to motivate students and promote learning through argumentation. We discussed the different types of serious games and the features that games should entail. We finally looked into their use in formal educational settings.

Work still needs to be done towards pinpointing the learning principles that will be used to guide and support our goal of fostering learning through the use of argumentative serious games. We have to take into account the fact that instructors will need to structure non-traditional situations, through which the classroom will become a community of learning. Future work directions also include the design, implementation and testing of the proposed argumentative serious game in various educational settings in both developed and developing coutries.

References

1. Osborne, J., Erduran, S., Simon, S.: Enhancing the quality of argumentation in school science. Journal of Research in Science Teaching 41(10), 994–1020 (2004)
2. Roschelle, J.M., Pea, R.D., Hoadley, C.M., Gordin, D.N., Means, B.M.: Changing how and what children learn in school with computer-based technologies. Children and Computer Technology 10(2), 76–101 (2000) (Electronic Version)
3. Veerman, A.L., Andriessen, J.E.B., Kanselaar, G.: Collaborative argumentation in academic education. Instructional Science 30, 155–186 (2002)
4. Kuhn, L., Kenyon, L.O., Reiser, B.J.: Fostering scientific argumentation by creating a need for students to attend to each other's claims and evidence. In: Proceedings of the 7th international Conference on Learning Sciences, pp. 370–375 (2006)
5. Hogan, K., Maglienti, M.: Comparing the epistemological underpinnings of student's and scientists' reasoning about conclusions. Journal of Research in Science Teaching 38(6), 663–687 (2001)
6. Gorlinsky, C., Serva, M.A.: Leveraging online gaming for teaching student leadership and teamwork. In: Proceedings of the special interest group on management information system's 47th annual conference on Computer personnel research, pp. 73–76. ACM, New York (2009)
7. Naylor, S., Keogh, B., Downing, B.: Argumentation and primary science. Research in Science Education 37, 17–39 (2007)
8. Susi, T., Johannesson, M., Backlund, P.: Serious Games: An Overview, Technical Report HS-IKI-TR-07-001, School of Humanities and Informatics, University of Skovde, Sweden (2007)
9. Mitchell, A., Savill-Smith, C.: The use of computer and video games for learning: A review of the literature. Learning and Skills Development Agency, London (2004)
10. Squire, K., Jenkins, H.: Harnessing the power of games in education. Insight 3(1), 5–33 (2003)

11. Squire, K., Steinkuehler, C.: Meet the Gamers: They Research, Teach, Learn, and Collaborate. So Far, without Libraries. Library Journal 130(7) (2005)
12. McFarlane, A., Sparrowhawk, A., Heald, Y.: Report on the educational use of games. TEEM, Department of Education and Skills (2008)
13. Jenkins, H., Klopfer, E., Squire, K., Tan, P.: Entering the education arcade. Comparative media studies, MIT. ACM Computers in Entertainment 1(1) (2003)
14. Prensky, M.: Digital Game-Based Learning. Paragon House (2007)
15. Erduran, S., Simon, S., Osborne, J.: TAPing into argumentation: Developments in the application of Toulmins argument pattern for studying science discourse. Science Education 88(6), 915–933 (2004)
16. Sandford, R.: Teaching with Games: COTS games in the classroom. In: The proceedings of JISC Innovating e-Learning 2006: Transforming Learning Experiences, online conference (2006)
17. Holland, W., Jenkins, H., Squire, K.: Theory by design. In: Perron, B., Wolf, M. (eds.) Video Game Theory, pp. 25–46. Routledge, New York (2003)
18. Gee, J.P.: What video games have to teach us about learning and literacy. Palgrave Macmillan, Basingstoke (2003)
19. Prensky, M.: Computer Games and Learning. In: Raessens, J., Goldstein, J. (eds.) Handbook of Computer Game Studies, pp. 97–122. MIT Press, Cambridge (2005)
20. Serious Games Initiative, `http://www.seriousgames.org`
21. Sandford, R., Ulicsak, M., Facer, K., Rudd, T.: Teaching with Games: Using commercial off-the-shelf computer games in formal education. Futurelab Final Report (2006)

Using Cell Phones to Improve Language Skills: The Hadeda Project

Laurie Butgereit, Adele Botha, and Daniel van Niekerk

Meraka Institute, CSIR
Pretoria, South Africa
lbutgereit@meraka.org.za,
abotha@meraka.org.za,
dvniekerk@csir.co.za

Abstract. Language skills are essential for education and economic development. Many countries (especially in Africa) have more than one official language and even more unofficial languages. Being able to express oneself effectively in the written word is required for tertiary education. Unfortunately, cell phones are often blamed for the degradation of language skills. There have been many studies blaming cell phone usage and instant messaging as being responsible for the the lack of language skills of children, teenagers, and young adults. Hadeda is a facility where teachers and parents can create spelling lists for pupils and children using either a cell phone or an internet based workstation. Hadeda then generates a fun and enjoyable cell phone midlet (computer program) which pupils and children can download onto their personal cell phone. Hadeda pronounces the words with electronic voices and the pupils and children can then practice their spelling on a medium they enjoy.

Keywords: cell phone, spelling, language.

1 Introduction

Language skills are essential for economic development. It has been shown that language skills have a direct impact on the employment and earning capabilities of individuals. This has been shown to be true in English[1] and non-English speaking countries[2] and in both first world and third world countries.

Unfortunately, the cell phone has been blamed for the degradation of language skills[3]. Teachers have lamented the lack of spelling skills with pupils who use cell phones, SMS (often called 'texting' in some English-speaking countries), and instant messaging[4].

Hadeda is an attempt to use the cell phone to help improve language skills. It is a facility which allows teachers and parents to create spelling lists in more than one human language. Hadeda then generates audio clips for the spelling words and packages them into a downloadable cell phone application (or midlet). The pupils and children can then download the midlet onto their own phone and practice their spelling.

A. Villafiorita, R. Saint-Paul, and A. Zorer (Eds.): AFRICOMM 2009, LNICST 38, pp. 11–19, 2010.

Hadeda is named after the Hadeda Ibis bird which is found throughout the grasslands and savannas of Africa[5]. It is a raucous, noisy bird making a distinctive haa-haa-haa-haaa-de-da sound. The name is appropriate for a cell phone application or midlet which makes lots of noise.

2 The Landscape

The cell phone is seen everywhere in Africa. Reports vary as to cell phone penetration on the African continent. The fact that cell phones are shared within a family, however, support the allegation that penetration is high[6].

Quality education, skilled teachers, school rooms, textbooks, paper and pencils, however, are not ubiquitous in Africa.

The question we originally asked was "Can the cell phone be used effectively in education?" Previous work we had done in using cell phones and mobile instant messaging to assist in mathematics education[7][8][9] was successful and encouraged us to now look at the potential use of cell phones in language education.

South Africa has a foot in both the first world and the third world – as does the rest of Africa. Teachers in private schools and government schools in middle class suburbs complain that cell phone spelling and instant messaging are destroying the English Language. While at the same time, pupils in rural schools often do not have competent English teachers.

Yet in both environments, the private school and the rural school, cell phones could be found.

Although the cell phone is everywhere, the capabilities of the cell phones vary. If Hadeda is to be successful, it must take into account the wide range of facilities offered on cell phones.

3 Overall Design of Hadeda

Hadeda consists of two major sections.

The first section is an internet website designed so that it can easily be accessed on a cell phone using either the cell phone browser or Opera Mini. This internet website allows teachers and parents to type in a list of spelling words. The website will then generate audio files of the words using an electronic voice. It will then package the electronic voices with the classes of a Java midlet and publish the midlet or Java application on the internet.

The second section of Hadeda is the Java midlet itself. The pupils will then download the Java midlet onto their personal (or their family) cell phone. The midlet will then speak to them their spelling words and the pupils or children will have to type in the spelling words on the cell phone keypad. Correct spelling will reward the pupils or children with a recording of the Hadeda shouting haa-haa-haa-haaa-de-da. Figure 1 shows a pictorial description of Hadeda.

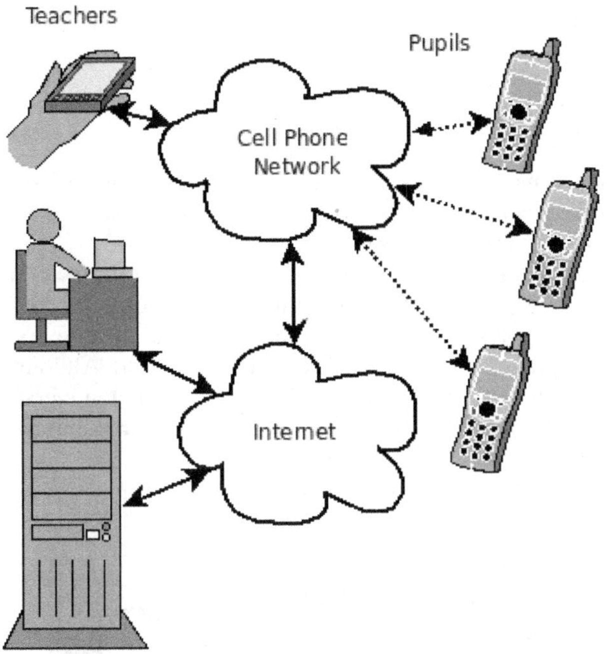

Fig. 1. The dotted line on the pupil cell phones is to indicate the temporary nature of that connection. It is only needed when the midlet is initially downloaded onto the cellphone.

A technical discussion of how this was achieved is discussed below.

4 Internet Website

The Hadeda internet website was created using a variety of open source and free tools.

The Tomcat servlet container was used for the teacher or parent side of Hadeda. It allows teachers or parents to login, create workspaces, and create spelling lists. The default Tomcat MemoryRealm was used for login security.

Java FreeTTS was used to generate the audio for English language words. The indigenous African voices (currently only isiXhosa although more will be available soon) are generated by a text-to-speech software developed at Meraka Institute (more specific detail on the indigenous voices is in section 9 below). Espeak was used for the similar purpose with the remaining languages (Afrikaans, Swahili, and all of the European languages). All three of these synthesizers generated WAV format audio files. WAV format, however, is not supported on all cell phones. In addition the WAV files generated by the synthesizers were often 5K for a simple two syllable words.

A combination of Sox and the AMR Codecs was used to convert the WAV format into AMR format which is playable on the majority of cell phones. Recordings of simple words such as "apple" were nearly 5.3K in WAV format and a mere 594 bytes when in AMR format. In view of the fact that midlets or Java cell phone applications have a size limitation, keeping the audio files as small as possible was important.

Once the Java midlet was generated, the Apache webserver was used to actually feed out the midlet to the pupils.

5 Java Midlet

The Java Midlet framework was originally developed using Sun's Wireless Toolkit. A collection of free or open source icons, images, and sounds were incorporated into the midlet to make the midlet enjoyable for children.

Specific care was taken to ensure that the midlet would run on a wide variety of cell phones including phones which had limited facilities. The midlet would internally query the phone on which it was running to find out the phone's facilities.

All images and icons were converted to PNG format. Although many modern phones can display images in JPEG and GIF format, it is not universal.

For Hadeda to be successful in helping children and pupils improve their language skills, it had to run on a wide variety of cell phones.

Figure 2 shows a typical cell phone running Hadeda.

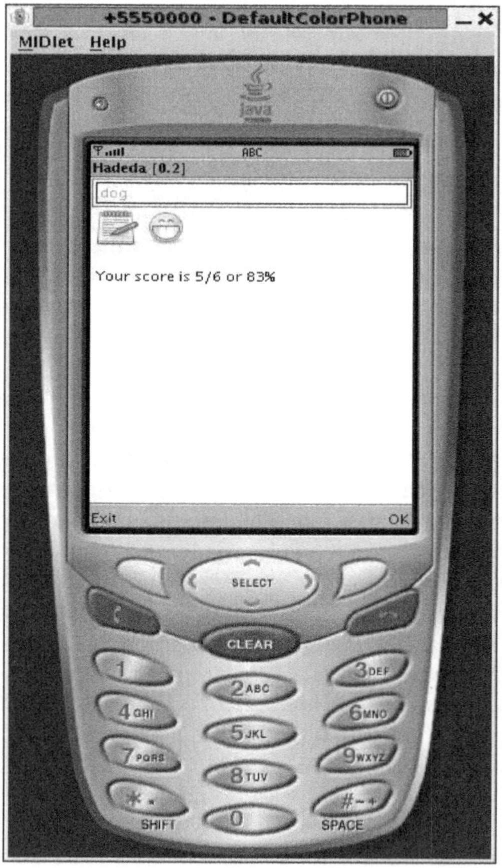

Fig. 2. A typical cell phone screen

6 Connectivity, Airtime and Costs

Throughout the design and implementation of Hadeda, an attempt was made to keep the costs to both the teachers and to the children to an absolute minimum.

Teachers or parents need to either be connected to the internet via an internet based workstation or via their cell phone in order to create the spelling lists.

Pupils or children need to be connected to the internet via their cell phone in order to download the midlet. Depending on the pupils' specific phone facilities, it could also be possible to send the midlet to the pupils' phones via BlueTooth. Thereafter, children or pupils could practice their spelling lists without incurring any additional airtime costs.

Typical internet costs for cell phones in South Africa are R2.00 (approximately thirty US cents) per megabyte. Typical sizes of spelling lists with 20 words with two syllables were under 100K giving a cost to the pupil of 20 South African cents (or approximately 3 US cents) to download the Java midlet.

The children would not incur any additional airtime costs after the spelling list midlet was downloaded onto their phones.

7 Ethics and Safety

Throughout the design and development process, we were continually aware that it would be minor children (some as young as 5 years old) who would be the end users of Hadeda. From the initial conception of Hadeda, the safety and well being of these children was paramount.

There were three important safety issues which we addressed

1. Teachers and parents who wanted to generate spelling lists needed to contact the authors of this paper in order to get permission to use our internet website. This was necessary because we did not want unsavoury adults to create spelling lists which had vocabulary which were not appropriate for minor children.
2. Any teacher or parent who abused this authority and generated spellings lists which were not appropriate could be easily removed from our server.
3. No personal information about the minor children was stored on any of our servers. While the pupil or child was, in fact, running the Hadeda midlet application on their phone, a running score or total was kept on the phone. This score, however, was removed when the midlet was finished.

8 Educational Issues

We have based our research on the extended activity framework [10] adapted from Engestrom's [11] extended activity model. From this our aim has been to support the activities of educators in their endeavors to teach or facilitate, and students in their endeavors to learn.

The drill and practice of spelling lists is founded in the Behaviorist theory. Greeno, Collins and Resnick [12] cluster this under the assumption of "learning as activity." Kearsley [13] identifies three fundamental principles common in behaviorist learning:

1. Positive reinforcement
2. Learning in small manageable blocks
3. Generalization of learning can produce secondary conditioning

Hadeda has incorporated these implicitly in its design and explicitly as a desired outcome in that fluency in spelling could produce secondary results in literacy. The learner is encouraged to drill and practice by presenting the spelling list with technology that they are familiar with and that is personal and motivational. The amount of words is limited to 20 to enable learners to complete a cycle in a relative short amount of time. The predictive spelling feature can support learners additionally in early stages of the practice.

Hadeda, as the result of the mobility of the technology, will facilitate group work as a face to face exercise in class context or individually as reinforcement.

9 Indigenous Voices

The implementation of the isiXhosa audio voice clips is based on work done by the Human Language Technologies research group at Meraka Institute. This relies on a number of core language resources and tools including:

- Data resources:
  - Text corpora
  - Speech corpora
  - Pronunciation models (in the form of grapheme-to-phoneme conversion rules) developed by using the Default&Refine algorithm [14] implemented in the DictionaryMaker software package [15].
- Software modules:
  - Natural language processing modules (e.g. language specific syllabification algorithms).
  - Synthesis engine (a modular synthesis framework and engine designed for multilingual environments named Speect [16] is used).
  - System development tools (software including automatic phonetic alignment capabilities optimized for scarce resourced environments [17]).

These resources and software modules are especially suited to developing technologies in resource scarce contexts such as South Africa.

The synthesizer uses the unit-selection synthesis approach and consequently the voice has a quality similar to the speech corpus it is based on. The runtime system follows the client-server model where the client sends a synthesis request including a language designation to the server which responds; synthesizing a waveform by applying the following the basic processes:

1. Text processing
2. Linguistic analysis
3. Waveform synthesis

In the case of this application all input is in the form of single words, thus this process reduces to grapheme to phoneme conversion, syllabification and unit selection and resynthesis from the acoustic database.

10 Pilots

Hadeda has had two formal pilots. The first was an English home language pilot in an English language primary school. The second was a German second language pilot in an English language secondary school.

The first pilot was at a private English speaking primary school in the North West province of South Africa. The school had a policy in place where children could bring their cell phones to school during the day but could not use them during school hours. The pilot was held at the end of the academic school year in South Africa and the school relaxed their cell phone policy for this pilot.

A number of technical issues were encountered during this pilot and Hadeda was modified to cater for these issues. These included:

1. A number of extremely old cell phones could not play any type of sound file. The pupils, however, were extremely enthusiastic and we modified Hadeda so that these pupils could view the spelling word on the screen for a few seconds. Hadeda would then erase the spelling word from the screen and the pupils would have to type in the spelling word on the cell phone keypad. This is similar to the old "pencil and paper" drill of practicing spelling words but just using a different medium.
2. A number of phone could not handle the diacritical marks on letters in words such as the Afrikaans "môre" or "sê". We discovered that such cell phones did not have the appropriate character sets loaded. We again modified Hadeda so that it would test the cell phone to see if the appropriate character sets were loaded. If not, the pupil could still type in the correct letters (without the diacritical marks) on the cell phone and Hadeda would print a large warning sign indicating that the diacritical marks were missing.

We also encountered a number of "softer" issues which were unrelated to the technicalities of Hadeda. These included:

1. Pupils are extremely attached to their cell phones. Many often view the cell phone as a part of themselves. A number of pupils felt embarrassed when Hadeda did not originally execute properly on their personal phones. One child actually cried when Hadeda would not run on her phone (although we did manage to get it running the next day). In future pilots, we will have some spare phones available for pupils to use in such cases.
2. Pupils are good at "viral marketing". During our original pilot, only a handful of pupils came to the first day of our pilot program. But as they told their friends about the pilot, more and more pupils arrived with signed consent forms and took part.
3. Older participants are always willing to help younger participants to configure their cell phones. In future pilots, we may consider having a pre-pilot

day to just train older pupils on the use and let them train the younger pupils the subsequent days.

Our second pilot was at a German second language class in an English speaking private secondary school. The only problem we encountered during this pilot was the use of the ß letter in German words. Our software mistakenly allowed pupils to type in the letter B instead of two s letters on cell phones which did not have the proper character sets loaded.

11 Conclusion

Preliminary results from informal testing indicate that Hadeda may have a positive impact on language skills learning; however, firm conclusions will not be available until after additional educational pilots.

12 The Way Forward

At the time of writing this paper, Hadeda can generate vocabulary spelling lists in English, French, Portuguese, German, Afrikaans, Swahili and isiXhosa. The basic technological framework allows other TTS voices to be used. In the near future we will be implemented another of South African's official languages developed by the Human Language Technologies research group at Meraka Institute.

References

1. Dustmann, C., Fabbri, F.: Language Proficiency and Labour Market Performance of Immigrants in the UK. The Economic Journal 113(489), 695–717
2. Rendon, S.: The Catalan premium: language and employment in Catalonia. Journal of Population Economics 20(3), 669–686
3. Yanzon, E.: Does Text Messaging Affect the Spelling Skills of Students? Far Eastern University English Language Journal 1, 33–37
4. Baron, N.: Instant Messaging and the Future of Language. Communications of the ACM 48(7), 29–30
5. Maclean, G.: Roberts Birds of Southern Africa, 5th edn., p. 74. CTP Book Printers, Cape (1984)
6. Ford, M., Batchelor, J.: From zero to hero – is the mobile phone a viable learning tool for Africa? In: 3rd International Conference on Social and Organisational Informations and Cybernetics, SOIC 2007, Orlando, USA, July 2007, p. 7 (2007)
7. Butgereit, L.: Math on Mxit: The Medium is the Message. In: 13th Annual National Congress of the Association for Mathematics Education of South Africa, p. 15
8. Butgereit, L.: Dr Math Rocks! Using Instant Messaging to Help Pupils with Mathematics Homework. In: IST-Africa 2008, Windhoek, Namibia (2008)
9. Butgereit, L.: Thumb Tribe Math Wars! In: 14th Annual National Congress of the Association for Mathematics Education of South Africa
10. Botha, A., Traxler, J., Marques, L., Isias Sedona, C., Sutinen, E.: More than Mobile. In: IST-Africa 2008, Windhoek, Namibia (2008)

11. Engestrom, Y.: Learning by Expanding: An Activity-Theoretical Approach to Development Research. Helsinki, Orienta-Konsultit Oy
12. Greeno, J., Collins, A., Resnick, L.: Cognition and Learning. Handbook of Educational Psycology. Simon & Schuster MacMillan, NY
13. Kearsley, G.: Explorations in learning and instruction: The theory into practice database, `http://tip.psychology.org` (retrieved March 14, 2008)
14. Davel, M., Barnard, E.: Pronunciation Prediction with Default & Refine. Computer Speech and Language 22, 374–393 (2008)
15. Davel, M., Barnard, E.: DictionaryMaker, `http://dictionarymaker.sourceforge.net`
16. Louw, J.A.: Speect: a multilingual text-to-speech system. In: Proceedings of the Nineteenth Annual Symposium of the Pattern Recognition Association of South Africa, Cape Town, South Africa, November 2008, pp. 165–168 (2008)
17. Van Niekerk, D.R., Barnard, E.: Phonetic alignment for speech synthesis in under-resourced languages. In: INTERSPEECH, Brighton, UK, pp. 880–883 (2009)

Mobile Learning Content Authoring Tools (MLCATs): A Systematic Review

Raymond Mugwanya[1] and Gary Marsden[2]

ICT4D Lab, Department of Computer Science, University of Cape Town, South Africa
ray.mugwanya@gmail.com, gaz@cs.uct.ac.za

Abstract. Mobile learning is currently receiving a lot of attention in the education arena, particularly within electronic learning. This is attributed to the increasing mobile penetration rates and the subsequent increases in university student enrolments. Mobile Learning environments are supported by a number of crucial services such as content creation which require an authoring tool. The last decade or so has witnessed increased attention on tools for authoring mobile learning content for education. This can be seen from the vast number of conference and journal publications devoted to the topic. Therefore, the goal of this paper is to review works that were published, suggest a new classification framework and explore each of the classification features. This paper is based on a systematic review of mobile learning content authoring tools (MLCATs) from 2000 to 2009. The framework is developed based on three broad dimensions i.e. Technology, Pedagogy and Usability and a number of features such as system type, development context, Tools and Technologies used, tool availability, ICTD relation, Multimedia support, tool purpose, support for standards, learning style support, intuitive Graphical User Interface and accessibility. This paper provides a means for researchers to extract assertions and several important lessons for the choice and implementation of MLCATs.

Keywords: Mobile Education, Content Authoring Tools, Systematic Review.

1 Introduction

Mobile and ubiquitous learning is emerging as the next generation of education environments. This is partly due to the high mobile penetration rates and subsequent increases in university student enrolments [11][44][55]. Therefore, learning demands from mobile devices are increasing thus presenting challenges for content creation [17][29]. In order to deal with these demands, quality content creation is of paramount importance. Authoring tools are the programs used by academics to create and distribute content in various domains [61]. A tool is considered to be a MLCAT if the resulting content can be consumed on mobile devices. The use of authoring tools is not a simple task for academics who wish to author electronic content [20][54]. This may be due to steep learning curve(s),

A. Villafiorita, R. Saint-Paul, and A. Zorer (Eds.): AFRICOMM 2009, LNICST 38, pp. 20–31, 2010.

some academics being technology shy and resistant to change or possibly inadequate institutional support. The goal of MLCATs is to empower academics (even the recalcitrant ones) to easily author content that is consumable on mobiles so as to provide anywhere, anytime learning. Over time, many researchers have made efforts to design and implement MLCATs thus there is great diversity in both commercial and non commercial tools [36]. These tools are developed with various goals and purposes in mind resulting in a variety of architectures. Some tools, for example, are used to author tests [61][44][3][40]), support content re-use [29] and support content authoring for integration with Learning Management Systems (LMS)[37][44][55] and present video lectures [25][47][48][64]among others. Numerous articles have been published in journals and conferences relating to MLCATs, suggesting a lot of interest in the design and implementation of innovative MLCATs. Therefore, we feel that this is a good time to review MLCATs. The aim of this paper is to classify and summarize research relevant to M-Learning content authoring tools, provide a framework for the integration and classification of articles and to derive suggestions for M-Learning researchers based on the review. The rest of this paper is organized as follows; section 2 details the procedure we followed to conduct the systematic review and outlines the characteristics of our primary studies, section 3 explores our classification framework while sections 4 and 5 detail the classification framework results, summary and conclusions respectively.

2 Procedure

Our primary studies were selected based on the keyword search *'mobile learning and content authoring tool*'* for the period 2000 to 2009, using eight online databases. A total of 142 articles were generated from our initial search. The number of articles by online database are as follows: ACM Digital Library (96), EBSCOHOST (Electronic Journal Service) (02), Emerald (03), GALE (04),

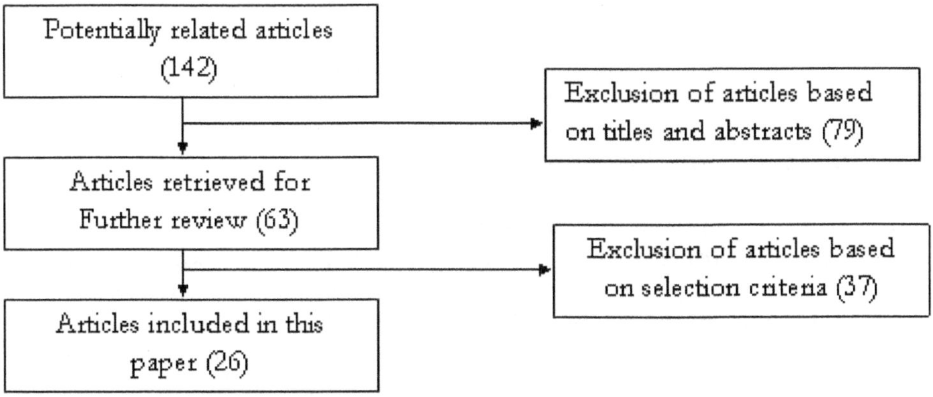

Fig. 1. Procedure for selection of articles

IEEE Xplore (08), Science Direct (05), Springer (02) and Google Scholar (21). A total of 79 articles were excluded based on their titles and abstracts. This was followed by a further inclusion/exclusion of articles based on whether they contained MLCAT literature as their core. 63 articles met the selection criteria and were presented for further review. 37 articles were then excluded because despite having relevant titles, abstracts and full text, they did not present relevant tools for this study.

2.1 Classification of MLCAT Articles by Publication Year

Figure 2 shows the number of MLCAT articles by publication year. It can be noted that from 2002 to 2005, there was an increase in articles published, with 2005 registering the highest number of articles. From then on, MLCAT publications declined by half in the 2006, 2007 period with a further slight decline in 2008 and 2009. This may be attributed to the fact that many published systems rarely move past the experimental stage and the need for universities to justify the case for investment in learning technologies. However, many published tools have been successfully used in the various contexts for which they have been developed.Therefore, we believe that the next decade will be characterized by increased interest and development of mobile learning content authoring tools.

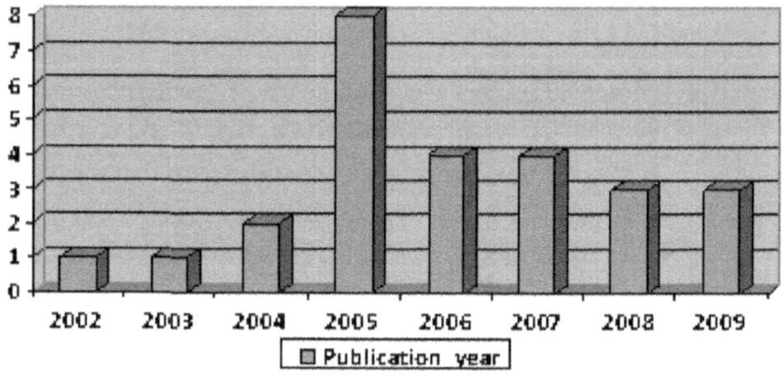

Fig. 2. Number of articles by publication year

3 Classification Framework

In this section, we present our classification framework which offers an analysis of MLCATs. According to [37][70] and a report by Taylor et al.on best practices for instructional design and content development for mobile learning, we identify three broad dimensions to classify MLCATs namely; technology, pedagogy and Usability. We feel that they constitute the necessary and sufficient attributes for the development or choice of adoption of MLCATs. Similarly, [9][70] suggest that technology is a critical enabler for mobile learning but the major challenges lie with content authoring, delivery strategy (Pedagogy), the need for a

GUI and accessibility support (Usability). We further sub-divide technological features (while providing their corresponding acronyms) as follows: system type (Sys Typ.), authoring techniques and technologies used (Techno.), tool Availability (Av.), ICTD relation (ICTD), tool purpose and Multimedia support (MM). Pedagogical requirements comprise of standards (Stds.) and learning style (LS) support whereas usability requirements include existence of an intuitive graphical user interface (GUI) and accessibility (Acc.).

We distinguish several system types i.e. artificial intelligence tools (A), traditional authoring tools that use hypertext and multimedia features for content creation (T), video capture systems (V) and natural language speaking and handwriting tools (N). Artificial intelligence tools enable academics to create intelligent tutoring systems in their domain of expertise through a graphical user interface. The tool then models student usage characteristics so as to provide them with individualized guidance during learning [61]. Video capture tools involve recording, encoding and streaming of the instructors presentations for consumption on various end devices [62] whereas natural language speaking and handwriting tools use recognition software to convert speech and hand written material into editable objects (i.e. text, video, audio or graphics) which are authored for presentation on end devices[35]. We also give an indication of whether a tool offers desktop authoring (DA), mobile authoring (MA), content distribution to mobile (DM), desktops (DD)or both (DMD) and use ?? for a lack of feature support.

The second dimension explores the authoring techniques and development environments used; for example, some tools use single authoring (S) a technique used to create a single version of content for adaptation to any given end device, Multiple authoring (M) which involves creation of several content versions for the different consumer devices and Flexible authoring (F) which involves the creation of both single and multiple authored content versions [37]. The development environments include, among others, J2ME, eXtensible Markup Language (XML), .NET framework and Synchronized Multimedia Integration Language (SMIL) among others. In the next dimension, we classify tools against their availability. This implies that a tool is either Web based (w), Client based (c), has a downloadable version available (d) or can be purchased (p). The fourth dimension classifies tools based on whether they are developed with a developing world (ICTD) context in mind. The developing world is faced with various challenges such as those of infrastructure, poverty, literacy and sparsity.

The last two dimensions classify tools based on their purpose and the multimedia supported. The tools explored are used to create learning content, multiple choice quizzes, tests and video lectures among others. In addition, the tools support various media elements such as video (v), text (t), audio (a) and images (i). Within the pedagogical arena, we explore two features i.e. standards and learning styles. There are various standards available for mobile learning content authoring such as the Sharable Content Object Reference Model (SCORM) [1] and the IMS Global Learning Consortium Question and Test Interoperability [21]. Moreover, support for learning style and activity of learners such visual, tactile and other learning theories should be taken into account during content authoring for m-learning. Therefore, we classify tools based on their support for standards and learning styles. Within the usability arena, we classify tools based on whether they have an intuitive graphical user interface and/or support accessibility(support for people with disabilities).

4 Results of Classification

A total of 26 tools have been classified as illustrated in Table 1 below revealing some interesting observations. From a technology perspective, the biggest number of MLCATs are traditional tools those that use hypertext and multimedia features for content creation [3][7][9][15][17][20] [29][36][42][44][50][51][55], followed by video recording tools [24][47][48][64], artificial intelligence tools [37][42] [61] and natural language processing tools [3]. The LMS concept has been successful in many universities. Therefore, as a result majority of the tools are developed with the goal of being integrated into Learning Management Systems. For example, [44] is designed for integration into the AHA! System, [55] into Moodle and [37] into the Context-based adaptive Mobile Learning Environment (CoMoLE). In addition, many of the tools have been developed for desktop authoring, with some also providing for mobile authoring [36][61] and the greatest number supporting distribution of content for access on both mobile devices (smart phones, iPods, cell phones, etc.) and computers.

Herzog et al. argue that video content is not mandatory in most learning environments due limitations such as the need for constant internet bandwidth availability. Therefore, it is still a challenge to implement video recording within LMS architectures. A number of video recording tools have emerged based on the initial innovations by Apple i.e. [64] which allows video lectures to be recorded and content delivered to mobile devices such as iPods. The resulting content cannot be later changed, implying single authoring. The majority of tools in our review use this authoring approach with [29][36] offering flexible authoring. We note that a vast number of tool articles do not give an indication of the authoring techniques used hence the use of ?? in our matrix. The natural language processing tools use hand-writing software, screen capture software and video streaming for content delivery and the matrix also reveals that majority of the tools are either web-based or client tools with only [55] having a demo version available whereas [64] can be purchased.

In much of the developing world, infrastructure is characterized by little or no internet bandwidth, unreliable and intermittent mains electricity and limited user expertise among others. This implies that the developing world context requires ICTD relevant tools. Majority of the tools explored are developed for user contexts in the developed world and thus do not represent the needs of academics and learners in the developing world. For instance in much of sub-Saharan Africa, despite the huge investments by universities on LMSs such as Blackboard and WebCT, the impact of their use has not been significant. Several programmes have been offered through distance education but still heavily rely on first generation print and second generation face-to-face lectures [11].

Table 1. Tool Classification Matrix showing MLCATs Vs Dimensions

Dim.	Technology						Pedagogy		Usability	
Tool	**Sys Typ.**	**Auth.Tech and Techno.**	**Av.**	**ICTD**	**Tool purpose**	**MM.**	**Stds.**	**LS**	**GUI**	**Acc.**
[29]	T,DA, DMD	F, XML, XSLT	w	No	learning content and tests	t, i, a, v	Yes	No	Yes	No
[46]	T,DA, DMD	S, Java and XML	w	No	adaptive tests	t, i	No	No	No	No
[61]	A, MA, DA, DMD	S, ASP.NET, VB.NET, Windows Server 2000+, IIS, RDBMS	w	No	adaptive content and tests	t, i	No	Yes(Intelligence)	No	No
[37]	A,DA, DMD	?, Java, XML	w	No	Learning content	t, i	No	Yes	Yes	No
[52]	T, DA, DMD	S, XML, XHTML, CSS	c	No	Learning content	t, i, a	No	No	Yes	No
[35]	N,DA, DMD	??, hand writing, screen capture.,video streaming software	??	Yes	Learning content	t, i, v	No	No	No	No
[25]	??, DA,DMD	??, XML	??	No	Learning content	t, i, v	No	Yes(Learning Activity)	??	No
[36]	T,MA, DM	F, Visual C++, Pocket PC2003 OS	??	No	Learning content	t, i, v	No	No	??	No
[57]	T, D,DA, DMD	??, XHTML, XML	d	No	Learning content	t,i, v	Yes	Yes	??	No
[3]	T, DA, DM	??, SMS	c	No	quizzes answered through SMS	t, i	No	No	No	No
[3]	T, DA, DM	??, Palmtop, e-mail, MMS	w	No	interactive learning tasks for learner groups	t, i, a	No	Yes	??	No
[3]	T, DA, DM	??, PocketPC	c	No	Multiple choice quizzes	t, i	No	No	??	No
[51]	T, D, DA, DMD	??, Java, XML, XHTML	w	No	Learning content	t, i, v	No	No	Yes	No
[7]	T, DA, DMD	??, XML, RFID, GPS	w	No	Learning content	t, i, a	No	No	Yes	No
[44]	T, D,DA, DMD	??, XML	w	No	exercises of different types	t, i	No	Yes	No	No
[17]	T, D, DA, DMD	??, C sharp, XML	??	No	Learning content	t, i	No	Yes	??	No
[42]	A, DA, D	??,XML, HTML, CSS	c	No	Learning content and Tests	t, i , a, v, hyperlinks	Yes	No	Yes	No
[64]	V, DMD	??, Streaming Server, SMIL, MPEG-4	p	No	Learning content	Video podcasts, t,i,a	Yes	No	No	No
[9]	T, DA, DMD	??, SMIL	w	No	multimedia content	t, i, a, v	??	No	Yes	No
[48]	V, DA, DMD	??, ??	??	No	Instant multimedia content	t, i, a	??	No	Yes	No
[62]	??, DA, DD	??, XML, XSLT Style Sheets, XHTML	w	No	multimedia content	t, i, a	??	No	??	No
[20]	??, DA, MA, DMD	??, Java	w	No	examples	t, i,v	No	No	Yes	No
[50]	??, DA, MA, DMD,	??, Java	w	No	Tests, assess-ment, collabora-tive activities	t, i,a	??	No	Yes	No
[24]	V, DMD	??, Java 2D, Java Media Frameworks	c	No	Creating video centered ed-ucational spaces	t, i,v	No	No	??	??
[15]	??, HTTP, WAP, Web Services	??	w	No	multimedia content	t, i, a, v	No	No	??	No
[47]	??, H.264, MPEG-4	??	??	No	multimedia content	t, i, a, v	No	No	No	No

In addition, many of the tools in our matrix are developed with the sole purpose of creating learning content [25][29][37][52] whereas others are for authoring adaptive tests [44][61], quizzes [3][42] and for authoring instant multimedia (i.e. podcasts, vodcasts) [47][48][64]. Therefore, the majority of tools generate various combinations of multimedia elements i.e. text and images [37][44][61], text, images and video [24][34][35] whereas others support most media types [9][29][42][47]. Within the pedagogical arena we explored support for standards and learning style. This is because these aspects greatly impact on content creation. Our review revealed that some tools offer support for standards such as the sharable content reference model (SCORM) or the Question and Test Interoperability (QTI) [29][42][55][64] whereas [3][17][25][44][55][61] offer support for learning styles. Finally, the usability dimension explores the availability of an intuitive graphical user interface (GUI) and support for accessibility which deals with the provision for people with learning disabilities to utilize the tools. [7][9][17][20][29][37][48][50][52] have GUIs built into the MLCATs whereas none of the tools offer support for accessibility.

5 Summary and Conclusions

Our review was organized with the purpose of providing a comprehensive overview of research on MLCATs. Therefore, we reviewed MLCATs and examined them using the technology, pedagogy and usability dimensions as presented in our cross-tabulation matrix. The paper was based on a literature review of MLCATs from 2000 to 2009 using a keyword index and article title search. Overall, we found that the research activity related to MLCATs increased dramatically up to 2005 and then decreased slightly from then on to 2009.

Our review provides literature on the use of MLCATs and avails some insights to researchers and practitioners for the design and choice of tool adoption. The framework offers some general development considerations for MLCATs and offers a classification of the various tools. We also realize the need for tools to be developed within the contexts of the users in order for successful adoption of these technologies. Many of the MLCATs explored do not use design approaches that involve real system users in context. Therefore, we need to develop MLCATs that represent the needs of users and empower them to author content for use in mobile environments. Moreover, the varieties of tool implementations explored are mainly technology driven. We feel that in order for them to satisfy their intended needs which is facilitate the learning process, tool implementations should follow an integrated approach that takes into account usability and pedagogical aspects. We believe that this will lead to better design, increased use and adoption of MLCATs.

Although considerable attention was given to the classification framework design, some limitations still exist. Firstly, some relevant articles might have been overlooked as much of the literature was selected based on a review of the title, keyword or abstract only. In addition, despite the fact that titles and abstracts in most cases describe the content quite well, we excluded many articles that did not explore MLCATs as their core. White papers, dissertations, magazines and many articles related to MLCATs were not reviewed as our focus was journal and conference articles which presumably represent the highest level of peer reviewed research. As a result seven online databases were searched for our review. We also used university subscribed online databases which were restricted in some cases. Future work requires the need to adapt learning activities to personalization of course content based on students model and learning styles, ability to track students progress in mobile environments, provide feedback mechanisms and improve interactivity. There is also need to study and align the relationship between authoring technology, pedagogy concerns, usability, the ability to create content using mobile devices without the need for additional processing and the need to empower academics who are the domain experts to easily create content without the need for intervention by tool experts.

Acknowledgements

Our thanks to the Hasso Plattner Institute Research School, University of Cape Town and the Faculty of Computing and IT, Makerere University for their support without which this work would not have been possible.

References

1. Advanced Distributed Learning Website, `http://www.adlnet.org/Pages/Default.aspx`
2. Anacleto, J.C., Carlos, A.J., de Carvalho, A.F., Dias, A.L.: Bridging the gap among cultures: the challenge faced by teachers on producing content for computer-aided education. In: Proceedings of the 26th Annual ACM international Conference on Design of Communication, SIGDOC 2008, ACM, New York (2008)
3. Attewell, J.: From Research and Development to Mobile Learning: Tools for Education and Training Providers and their Learners. In: Proceedings of mLearn (2005), `http://www.mlearn.org.za/CD/papers/Attewell.pdf`
4. Brown, E., Cristea, A., Stewart, C., Brailsford, T.: Patterns in Authoring of Adaptive Educational Hypermedia: A Taxonomy of Learning Styles. Educational Technology and Society 8(3), 77–90 (2005)
5. Berlanga, A.J., García, F.J.: Authoring tools for adaptive learning designs in computer-based education. In: Proceedings of the 2005 Latin American Conference on Human-Computer interaction, vol. 24, pp. 190–201. ACM, New York (2005)
6. Bhaskar, N.U., Govindarajulu, P.: Essential Aspects of Learning content Development in Context Aware and Adaptive Mobile Learning Applications. International Journal of Computer Science and Network Security 9(1), 339–346 (2009)
7. Broll, G., Rukzio, R., Björn, W.: Authoring Support for Mobile Interaction with the Real World. In: Pervasive Late Breaking Results, Toronto, Ontario, Canada (2007); Bianchi, M.: Automatic video production of lectures using an intelligent and aware environment. In: Proceedings of the 3rd international Conference on Mobile and Ubiquitous Multimedia, vol. 83. ACM, New York (2004)
8. Bianchi, M.: Automatic video production of lectures using an intelligent and aware environment. In: Proceedings of the 3rd international Conference on Mobile and Ubiquitous Multimedia, vol. 83. ACM, New York (2004)

9. Bulterman, D.C., Hardman, L.: Structured multimedia authoring. ACM Trans. Multimedia Comput. Commun. Appl. 1, 89–109 (2005)
10. Collins, T.G.: English Class on the Air: Mobile Language Learning with Cell Phones. In: Proceedings of the Fifth IEEE International Conference on Advanced Learning Technologies, p. 1 (2005)
11. Ngugi, C., Irungu, N., Muwonge, B., Langa, P.V., Pederson, J., Butcher, N., Hoosen, S., Moll, I., Adam, F., Backhouse, J., Mhlanga, E., Kouame, G., Tolba, A., Mutti, B., Eden, C.: Status Report on ICTs and Higher Education in Africa. Published by the Centre of Educational Technology, University of Cape Town, SA (2007)
12. Chandra, S.: Lecture video capture for the masses. SIGCSE Bull. 39, 3 (2007)
13. Cebeci: Using podcasts as audio learning objects. Interdisciplinary Journal of Knowledge and Learning Objects 1552-2210, 2, 47 (2006)
14. Chu, W. C., Lin, H., Chen, J., Lin, X., Lau, R.W.H.: Context-sensitive content representation for mobile learning. In: Lau, R., Li, Q., Cheung, R., Liu, W. (eds.) ICWL 2005. LNCS, vol. 3583, pp. 349–354. Springer, Heidelberg (2005)
15. de, F., Santos, H., Santana, L.H., Martins, D.S., De Souza, W.L., do Prado, A.F., Biajiz, M.: A ubiquitous computing environment for medical education. In: Proceedings of the 2008 ACM Symposium on Applied Computing, pp. 1395–1399. ACM, New York (2008)
16. Friedland, G., Hürst, W., Knipping, L.: Educational multimedia systems: the past, the present, and a glimpse into the future. In: Proceedings of the international Workshop on Educational Multimedia and Multimedia Education, pp. 1–4. ACM, New York (2007)
17. Gugerbauer, E.: Analysis of the Profit of M-Learning and A Framework for Authoring Mobile Learning Content, `http://www.tk.uni-linz.ac.at/download/gugerbauer.pdf`
18. Hürst, W., Welte, M., Jung, S.: An evaluation of the mobile usage of e-lecture podcasts. In: Proceedings of the 4th international Conference on Mobile Technology, Applications, and Systems and the 1st international Symposium on Computer Human interaction in Mobile Technology, pp. 16–23. ACM, New York (2007)
19. Herzog, M. A., Trier, M., Sieck, J.: Production engineering for video based e- and m-learning content. In: 10th Baltic Region Seminar on Engineering Education? 2006 UICEE Szczecin, Poland, pp. 1–4 (2006)
20. Hsiao, I., Li, Q., Lin, Y.: Educational social linking in example authoring. In: Proceedings of the Nineteenth ACM Conference on Hypertext and Hypermedia, pp. 229–230. ACM, New York (2008)
21. IMS Content Packaging Specification v1.1.3, `http://www.imsglobal.org/content/packaging/`
22. IMS Global Learning Consortium – Question and Test Interoperability, `http://www.imsglobal.org/question/version2.0`
23. IEEE Standard for Learning Object Metadata, `http://ltsc.ieee.org/wg12`
24. Jiang, H., Viel, A., Bajaj, M., Lue, R.A., Shen, C.: CThru: exploration in a video-centered information space for educational purposes. In: Proceedings of the 27th international Conference on Human Factors in Computing Systems, pp. 1247–1250. ACM, New York (2009)
25. Juang, Y., Chen, Y., Chen, Y., Chan, T.: Design of Learning Content Development Framework and System for Mobile Technology Enhanced Environment. In: Proceedings of the IEEE International Conference on Advanced Learning Technologies, pp. 1–3 (2004)

26. Jokela, T.: Authoring Toos for Mobile Multimedia Content. In: ICME, pp. 637–640 (2003)
27. Karampiperis, P., Sampson, D.: Designing learning systems to provide accessible services. In: Proceedings of the international Cross-Disciplinary Workshop on Web Accessibility (W4a), vol. 88, pp. 72–80. ACM, New York (2005)
28. Karampiperis, P., Sampson, D.: Designing learning services: from content-based to activity-based learning systems. In: Special interest Tracks and Posters of the 14th international Conference on World Wide Web, pp. 1110–1111. ACM, New York (2005)
29. Kuo, Y., Huang, Y.: MEAT: An authoring tool for generating adaptable learning resources (Mobile E-Learning Authoring Tool) (Report). Journal of Educational Technology and Society 51(18) (2009); Academic One File
30. Lichtschlag, L., Karrer, T., Borchers, J.: Fly: a tool to author planar presentations. In: Proceedings of the 27th international Conference on Human Factors in Computing Systems. ACM, New York (2009)
31. Leitner, M., Wolkerstorfer, P., Sefelin, R., Tscheligi, M.: Mobile multimedia: identifying user values using the means-end theory. In: Proceedings of the 10th international Conference on Human Computer interaction with Mobile Devices and Services, pp. 167–175. ACM, New York (2008)
32. Lara, E.d., Kumar, R., Wallach, D.S., Zwaenepoel, W.: Collaboration and multimedia authoring on mobile devices. In: Proceedings of the 1st international Conference on Mobile Systems, Applications and Services, pp. 287–301. ACM, New York (2003)
33. Lanir, J., Booth, K.S., Tang, A.: MultiPresenter: a presentation system for (very) large display surfaces. In: Proceeding of the 16th ACM international Conference on Multimedia, pp. 519–528. ACM, New York (2008)
34. Low, B.: Packaging educational content using IMS specifications. VINE 32(2) (2002)
35. Luciano, C., Guisseppe, S.: Pen-based tools for the creation of handwritten learning content. In: IEEE First International Workshop on Pen-Based Learning Technologies - Enabling Advanced Graphical, Multimodal and Mobile Learning Interactions, pp. 133–136 (2007)
36. Li, S., Kim, S., Kim, S.: Collaborative MPEG-4 Contents Authoring, Presentation and Interaction in a Mobile Environment. In: Proceedings of the Sixth International Conference on Parallel and Distributed Computing, Applications and Technologies, pp. 1–5 (2005)
37. Martín, E., Carro, R.M.: Supporting the Development of Mobile Adaptive Learning Environments: A Case Study. IEEE Transactions on Learning Technologies 2(1), 23–36 (2009)
38. MobiLearn IST-2001-37187, `http://www.mobilearn.org/standards/standards.htm`
39. MOT, `http://wwwis.win.tue.nl/~acristea/mot.html`
40. Metso, M., Koivisto, A., Sauvola, J.: A Content Model for the Mobile Adaptation of Multimedia Information. The Journal of VLSI Signal Processing 29 (2001)
41. McFarlane, A., Williams, J.M., Bonnett, M.: Assessment and multimedia authoring a tool for externalising understanding. Journal of Computer Assisted Learning 16(3), 201–212 (2000)
42. Kravcik, M., Specht, M.: Authoring Adaptive Courses: ALE APPROACH. Advanced Technology for Learning 1(4) (2004), `actapress.com`

43. Näsänen, J., Oulasvirta, A., Lehmuskallio, A.: Mobile media in the social fabric of a kindergarten. In: Proceedings of the 27th international Conference on Human Factors in Computing Systems, pp. 2167–2176. ACM, New York (2009)
44. Proske, A., Narciss, S., Korndle, H.: The Exercise Format Editor. A Multimedia Tool for the Design of Multiple Learning Tasks (2002), http://studierplatz2000.tu-dresden.de/lehrlern/pdf/artikel/ef_editor02.pdf
45. Röüling, G., Trompler, C., Mühlhäuser, M., Köbler, S., Wolf, S.: Enhancing classroom lectures with digital sliding blackboards. In: Proceedings of the 9th Annual SIGCSE Conference on innovation and Technology in Computer Science Education, pp. 218–222. ACM, New York (2004)
46. Romero, C., Ventura, S., Hervas, C., De Bra, P.: An Authoring Tool for Building Both Mobile Adaptable Tests and Web Based Adaptive or Classic Tests. In: Wade, V.P., Ashman, H., Smyth, B. (eds.) AH 2006. LNCS, vol. 4018, pp. 203–212. Springer, Heidelberg (2006)
47. Roesler, V., Husemann, R., Costa, C.H.: A new multimedia synchronous distance learning system: the IVA study case. In: Proceedings of the 2009 ACM Symposium on Applied Computing, pp. 1765–1770. ACM, New York (2009)
48. Rubegni, E., Sabiescu, A., Paolini, P.: OneThousandAndOneStories: a format for multichannel multimedia narratives. In: Abascal, J., Fajardo, I., Oakley, I. (eds.) Proceedings of the 15th European Conference on Cognitive Ergonomics: the Ergonomics of Cool interaction, vol. 369, pp. 1–2. ACM, New York (2008)
49. Rößling, G., Joy, M., Moreno, A., Radenski, A., Malmi, L., Kerren, A., Naps, T., Ross, R.J., Clancy, M., Korhonen, A., Oechsle, R., Iturbide, J.Á.: Enhancing learning management systems to better support computer science education. SIGCSE Bull. 40(4), 142–166 (2008)
50. Sá, M., Carriço, L.: Handheld devices for cooperative educational activities. In: Proceedings of the 2006 ACM Symposium on Applied Computing, pp. 1145–1149. ACM, New York (2006)
51. Smith, S.: Creating Mobile Learning? (2006), http://www.handheldlearning.co.uk/hl2006/present/stuartsmith.pdf
52. Simon, R., Wegscheider, F., Tolar, K.: Tool-supported single authoring for device independence and multimodality. In: Proceedings of the 7th international Conference on Human Computer interaction with Mobile Devices and Amp; Services, vol. 111, pp. 91–98. ACM, New York (2005)
53. Sharda, N.K.: Authoring educational multimedia content using learning styles and story telling principles. In: Proceedings of the international Workshop on Educational Multimedia and Multimedia Education, pp. 93–102. ACM, New York (2007)
54. Tortora, G., Sebillo, M., Vitiello, G., D'Ambrosio, P.: A multilevel learning management system. In: Proceedings of the 14th international Conference on Software Engineering and Knowledge Engineering, vol. 27, pp. 541–547. ACM, New York (2002)
55. Tai, Y., Ting, R. Y.: Authoring Tools in e-Learning: A Case Study. In: Seventh IEEE International Conference on Advanced Learning Technologies, pp. 1–3 (2007)
56. The International Telecommunications Union Website (Market Information and Statistics), http://www.itu.int/ITU-D/ict/statistics/ict/index.html
57. The SourceForge.Net Website: eXeLearning Tool, http://apps.sourceforge.net/trac/exe/wiki
58. Teng, C., Chu, H., Wu, C.: mProducer: Authoring Multimedia Personal Experiences on Mobile Phones. In: IEEE International Conference on Multimedia and Expo., pp. 1251–1254 (2004)

59. Turban, G., Mühlhäuser, M.: A framework for the development of educational presentation systems and its application. In: Proceedings of the international Workshop on Educational Multimedia and Multimedia Education, pp. 115–118. ACM, New York (2007)
60. Van Dam, A., Becker, S., Simpson, R.M.: Next-generation educational software: why we need it and a research agenda for getting it. In: ACM SIGGRAPH 2007 Courses, p. 32. ACM, New York (2007)
61. Virvou, M., Alepis, E.: Mobile Educational Features in Authoring Tools for Personalised Tutoring. Computers and Education 44(1), 53–68 (2005)
62. Valverde-Albacete, F.J., Pedraza-Jiménez, R., Cid-Sueiro, J., Molina-Bulla, H., Díaz-Pérez, P., Navia-Vázquez, A.: InterMediActor: an environment for instructional content design based on competences. In: Proceedings of the 2003 ACM Symposium on Applied Computing, pp. 575–579. ACM, New York (2003)
63. Weal, M.J., Hornecker, E., Cruickshank, D.G., Michaelides, D.T., Millard, D.E., Halloran, J., De Roure, D.C., Fitzpatrick, G.: Requirements for in-situ authoring of location based experiences. In: Proceedings of the 8th Conference on Human-Computer interaction with Mobile Devices and Services, vol. 159, pp. 121–128. ACM, New York (2006)
64. Wolf, K., Linckels, S., Meinel, C.: Teleteaching anywhere solution kit (Tele-TASK) goes mobile. In: Proceedings of the 35th Annual ACM SIGUCCS Conference on User Services, pp. 366–371. ACM, New York (2007)
65. Zhang, C., Rui, Y., Crawford, J., He, L.: An automated end-to-end lecture capture and broadcasting system. ACM Trans. Multimedia Comput. Commun., 1–23 (2008)
66. Ihamäki, H., Vilpola, I.: Electronic Journal on e-Learning 2(1) (2004), `http://www.ejel.org/volume-2/vol2-issue1/issue1-art18-ihamaki-vilpoloa.pdf`
67. Adell, J., Castellet, J.M., Gumbau, J.P.: Selection of an open source virtual learning environment for Universitat JaumeI (2004), `http://cent.uji.es/doc/eveauji_en.pdf`
68. Nielsen, J.: Finding usability problems through heuristic evaluation, pp. 373–380. ACM Press, New York (1992)
69. Leung, C., Chan, Y.: Mobile Learning: A New Paradigm. In: Electronic Learning Proceedings of the 3rd IEEE International Conference on Advanced Learning Technologies, pp. 1–5 (2003), `http://www.te.ugm.ac.id/~widyawan/mobilearn/MobilearnParadigm.pdf`
70. Taylor, J., Bo, G., Bernazzani, R., Sharples, M.: WP4 - Pedagogical Methodologies and Paradigms (2005), `http://www.mobilearn.org/download/results/public_deliverables/MOBIlearn_D4.2_Final.pdf`

A Rural Implementation of a 52 Node Mixed Wireless Mesh Network in Macha, Zambia

Jonathan Backens[1], Gregory Mweemba[2], and Gertjan van Stam[3]

[1] Old Dominion University, Norfolk VA 23529, USA
jback006@odu.edu
[2] LinkNet, Macha, Zambia
gregory.mweemba@link.net.zm
www.link.net.zm
[3] Macha Works, Macha, Zambia
gertjan.vanstam@machaworks.org
www.machaworks.org

Abstract. In spite of increasing international and academic attention, there remains many challenges facing real world implementations of developing technologies. There has been considerable hype behind Wireless Mesh Networking as the ubiquitous solution for rural ICT in the developing world. In this paper, we present the real world rural mesh network implementation in the village of Macha, Zambia and draw both performance conclusions as well as overall experiential conclusions. The purpose of this paper is to introduce and analyze our low cost solution and extrapolate future trends for rural ICT implementations in Zambia.

Keywords: Wireless Mesh Network, Rural ICT, Implementation Test Case.

1 Introduction

The community owned and run LinkNet Multipurpose Cooperative Society services the rural community of Macha, Zambia with innovative communication technology and locally trained talent [8]. Since inception its model for connecting rural Zambia with ICT services has been to empower the local community to run and maintain a locally built, locally maintained and locally managed internet infrastructure based on wireless communication technologies. Utilizing only local talent and supplies, the Macha Network has provided not only a powerful and inspiring local ICT project, but has laid the foundation for a comprehensive test bed for other rural implementations. This real world solution consisting of a network of 52 Mesh Nodes and 99 total active wireless service providing devices remains one of the largest locally run rural networks in Africa.

In order to understand the conditions of Macha Zambia and a bit of the demands for ICT, it is important to consider the overall environment. Zambia as a country is the 17th lowest country on the UNDP's Human Development Index [3]. It consists primarily of agricultural workers with an average income

A. Villafiorita, R. Saint-Paul, and A. Zorer (Eds.): AFRICOMM 2009, LNICST 38, pp. 32–39, 2010.

of about $1USD/Day. The village of Macha is located in the Choma District of Southern Zambia, in a semi arid flat farming area. It remains 70 km from the nearest tarred road or landline phone. Currently there is a population of $\geq$ 135.000 persons within an 35 km radius[13]. As far as traditional mobile communications, GSM service arrived in December 2006 but as with much of rural Africa outages are common. Currently internet connectivity is available via VSAT, GSM EDGE and Short Wave although all are subject to cost, weather and power fluctuations(see Section 2.3 for more on challenges).

The main feature of Macha is the Macha Mission Hospital(MMH) and Malaria Institute at Macha(MIAM)[4]. These institutions provide health care for the greater Macha area as well as being the primary employer of educated professionals and medical researchers.

LinkNet(currently structured under Macha Works) began providing broadband internet service in 2006 to hospital professionals' residences, the MIAM clinic/lab and the local community center for an internet cafe. The motivation behind the Macha Network is nearly as diverse as its client base. The MIAM research laboratory and offices use the network for research, correspondence and data management, the Macha Mission Hospital utilizes similar resources in addition to e-health advances such as the Zambian Ministry of Health SmartCare program for digital health records. In addition, the local community exploits the Internet for e-learning with several community members attending online university courses [15]. Also, local farmers are discovering the power of the internet in understanding crop diversification[17].

This paper provides an overview of the entire Macha Network, benchmark testing of one of it implemented mesh networks, analysis of the viability of our current open source WIFI based mesh solutions in rural environments and conclusions about our implementation including challenges This paper builds on the foundational work by Matthee et al. in [14] where the Macha Network and vision for rural ICT development was first published. In this paper we illustrate the progress that has been made in the development and management of a large rural wireless network. In addition we extend conclusions drawn by the technical discussion of the Macha Network by Backens et al. in [9] to draw some conclusions on the feasibility of our solution in other deployments.

The paper is organized as follows, In Section II the overall technical implementation of the Macha Network is presented with a focus on the Wireless Mesh Network performance. Then in Section III we look at the challenges and lessons learned from our approach. Section IV we will discuss the future of our rural ICT development model expansion. Finally, Section V will draw conclusions about our rural ICT implementation model and subsequent 52 Node Wireless Mesh Network.

2 Network Description

The Macha Network employs a diverse group of low cost and readily available equipment for providing network coverage to the 100-150 daily network users.

Table 1. Wireless Devices in Macha Network

	MIAM	MMH	Other
Freifunk Mesh Nodes	11	0	14
Open-Mesh Nodes	0	27	0
Open WRT APs	8	17	4
Linksys Firmware APs	10	2	0
X-lin (directional)	0	0	6
TOTAL MESH NODES	**52**		
TOTAL APs	41		
TOTAL Linksys WRT54Gx	66		
TOTAL WIRELESS DEVICES	**99**		

These users and the subsequently associated networks are broken up into three basic groups: MIAM Campus, MMH residential housing and everyone else. As shown in Table 1, the Macha Network utilizes mostly Linksys WRT54GL wireless routers flashed with OpenWrt [6] based firmware (Freifunk[2] for Mesh and DD-WRT[1] for Access Points). An Open Mesh network is deployed within the hospital staff housing and consists of 27 Open-Mesh Mini-Router[5] nodes running its own firmware. In contrast, the hybrid mesh nodes consist of two WRT54GL boxes wired together with one serving as a mesh backbone node and the other as an Access Point (AP). These hybrid nodes can be seen in Fig. 1. The combination nodes are employed within the MIAM campus and are placed inside each residence in a unique indoor-to-indoor deployment method to provide coverage for the entire complex. Thus each house within the MIAM campus is outfitted with a hybrid mesh node and each house in the MMH campus is outfitted with an Open Mesh box. These nodes are deployed regardless of usage by the household so that overall coverage can be achieved. This also has the benefit of allowing easy connection of new users if at a later time the need arises.

Fig. 1. MIAM Hybrid Node: WMN + AP

Each of the three primary networks are fed from a central tower within in the MIAM complex. This central tower is located next to the IT Room which monitors and manages the network as well as maintains the gateway connection to the internet via VSAT. The gateway is connected via C-Band VSAT with CIR of 128 kbps burstable to 1 Mbps and a Ku-Band VSAT with 32 kbps burstable to 256 kbps.

It should also be noted that in addition to the WRT54GL boxes, the Macha Networks also utilizes locally available X-Lin outdoor wireless APs with directional antennas to feed the different networks from the central mast. Although readily available in Lusaka, these devices are imported into Zambia cheaply and have no known English benchmarks or technical data sheets.

2.1 Performance Conclusions

The Macha Mesh Network at MIAM represents a very typical 11 node Wireless Mesh Network deployment following the Meraka DIY guide [7] and the previously listed hardware. The primary concerns of the network was behavior in terms of latency and overall throughput. Since nodes were supplying the primary means of communications to many of these points it was essential that a adequate throughput and latency be maintained across all nodes in order to assure some level of QoS. Initial testing show in Figure 2. revealed that the overall latency was not affected in a great deal by the hop count from the gateway. In fact nearly all nodes experienced between 5-10ms of delay: a value well within the required QoS for most applications. It should be noted however that occasionally nodes would experience severe latency increases for brief periods. These were attributed to both the dynamic nature of the spectrum as well as the overall inefficiency of the OLSR routing of the Freifunk nodes.

In contrast to relatively promising latency performance, the MIAM network's throughput was shown to decrease at a better than linear rate inversely proportional to the number of hops away from the gateway(as seen in figure 2(b)). Although testing was done in a saturated worst-case network and typical performance can be markedly better, these results clearly show the limitations of our current wireless mesh network solutions in terms of network size per gateway. Although there have been better performances shown in laboratory tests with OLSR based wireless mesh networks in [11], the harsh real world conditions in rural Zambia have proved a limiting factor for our indoor to indoor approach.

Clearly broadband over indoor-to-indoor deployed mesh networks is not possible under our current technology constraints in the rural environment. However reasonable data rates are achievable for basic network usage by local users. This conclusion is pivotal in the argument for continued use of these hybrid mesh nodes in indoor to indoor deployments. In addition we are spurred on by the promising developments in mesh technology such as the development of better routing protocols such as B.A.T.M.A.N. which in lab tests have shown marked improvement over our OLSR approach [10].

In addition to overall performance, a more thorough analysis was conducted to compare the traditionally used 802.11b with DSSS to the 802.11g with OFDM to perhaps gain insight into additional throughput and latency factors. The initial testing was a simple comparison of 802.11b and 802.11g modes of operation based on similar static data rates. It was clear that although 802.11g employs the

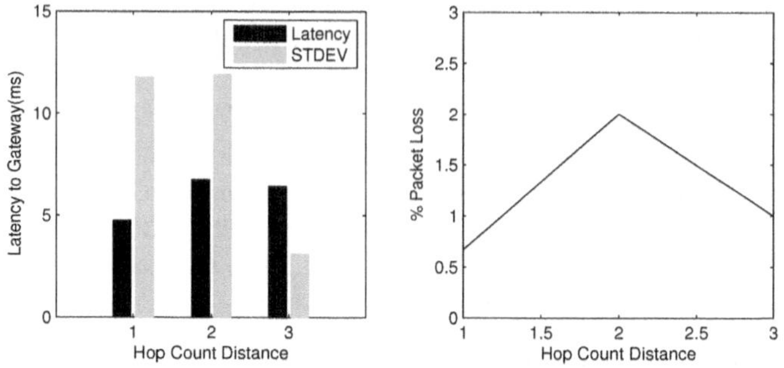

(a) MIAM Mesh Latency

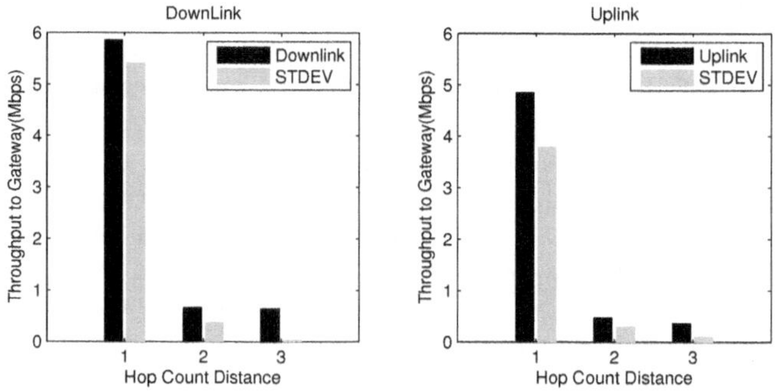

(b) MIAM Mesh throughput w/ default settings

Fig. 2. MAIM Mesh Performance

interference reducing OFDM modulation scheme and higher possible bit rates, that in a mesh environment these techniques were ineffective. In fact the 802.11b's DSSS modulation was shown to be far more stable and have a higher throughput with lower jitter than 802.11g OFDM in a Freifunk mesh deployment. 802.11gs higher throughput rates of 54Mbps were unachievable due to unacceptably high interference. (SNR too low to achieve connection in mesh configuration) A more detailed analysis is presented by Backens et al. in [9].

Although these performance conclusions highlight the considerable room for improvement in current mesh techniques, practically the limiting factor in network remains the Gateway connection under current conditions. The prohibitively high cost of our limited bandwidth(1Mbps connection) and its unavoidable latency ($\geq$400ms) remain the dominating characteristic of our network. However, from a user perspective the results of the Macha Network implementation and testing was encouraging. The network provides a usable and easily deployable solution for rural implementations. For small to medium sized mesh networks, the indoor to indoor model is possible, but can be greatly improved with better routing techniques, multiple gateways and adaptive modulation schemes.

2.2 Training

One of the surprising conclusions discovered throughout the LinkNet implementation in Macha is that installation and configuration of the initial wireless mesh technology is the smallest effort in developing a sustainable rural wireless network both in terms of cost and time. The dynamic nature of the wireless spectrum, the inconsistent performance of low cost hardware and difficulties of remote management combine to make create continual technical attention. However the greatest time and cost consumer remains in the training of local talent to undertake these tasks.

Simply stated, rural environments in underdeveloped countries by their very nature have little or no locally knowledgeable talent in the areas of wireless communication and networking. Rural talent almost universally has challenges with advanced topics such as protocol stacks, wireless propagation and troubleshooting processes. Topics that take time to understand and master even in developed countries. These same challenges have been faced in similar rural wireless mesh projects in India [16] and South Africa [12]. Therefore holistic training in Macha has been implemented though both the development of LinkNet Information Technology Academy and extensive self-motivated study. Originally LinkNet employed exclusively self-motivated study by providing apt future technicians and engineers free internet access and refurbished hardware to learn on. The initial results were very promising as exposure to the vast learning resources of the Internet and a few helpful practice parts produced 4 well qualified computer technicians. However as more wireless networking was introduced into Macha and specifically mesh networking, it became obvious that formal training would be required to fill in the holes in self-study education.

LinkNet takes advantage of a bevy of interim knowledge as scholars and IT experts visit Macha to supplement the core networking and computer maintenance coursework. This education has drastically increased the numbers of qualified technicians and helped improve the wireless expertise of the local talent. In addition now only occasional technical issues arise that are beyond the knowledge of local talent.

Our experience has shown that clearly, a locally trained workforce capable of managing a substantial wireless mesh network is possible but may require months of training and experience.

2.3 Challenges

The Macha implementation has faced many challenges with both equipment and environment. One of the most detrimental obstacles in rural Zambia remains the prohibitive cost of VSAT internet. Current LinkNet allocates nearly 2.000 USD/Month for its VSAT connections which are almost constantly saturated with traffic. Increasingly difficulties are foreseeable in the near future as regardless of funding, there is becoming a shortage of available channels and bandwidth on existing satellites. Thus the most expensive Internet in the world is becoming even more so.

Similar to other rural African projects, Macha struggles with regular power issues. Weekly power outages, spikes, brownouts, sags and lightning strikes are infrequent in most developed areas, but are commonplace in rural Zambia. Often these can result in unusual network behavior as equipment put in unstable states as well as high rates of equipment failure. One such example is the 27 node Open-Mesh deployment which fails to recover from certain low power conditions and requires manual resetting each node. This is a labor intensive task during raining season since it can occur on a daily basis.

Another common problem is the lack of quality equipment. Since many commercial and high-end products are not available or affordable, the Macha network has been built with locally available products which have a wide range of quality and documentation. One example of this are the X-Lin WIFI directional APs which are non-upgradable and are non-interoperable with Linksys WRT54Gx's even though both claim IEEE 802.11 compliance.

3 Future Work

LinkNet under the Macha Works oversight is committed to expanding ICT deployments to over 10 rural communities in 2010. This requires significant standardizing of the design and large scale role out of hybrid mesh networks. We are moving beyond proof of concept and evaluation and into production. In addition, the focus is moving from multi-specialist research in wireless mesh networking (primarily expatriate initiated) into inter-disciplinary research. As we have discovered the broad extent of influence rural ICT and community networks have in Macha, we are left seeking to integrate multi-specialist research, with development truly out of local need.

The many obstacles in local talent training and the required time investment has lead LinkNet to attempt the deskilling of mesh network roll out and maintenance engineering. This simplification would allow for quicker deployments and correlate with our values of empowering locally trained rural talent. Furthermore we are partnering with national African research and education institutions to develop further research areas.

Lastly, we are joining in the development of rural community ICT business models. This is currently a hot topic of research within the development community and Macha Works is seeking to help provide a equal contribution funding model.

4 Conclusions

The Hybrid Macha Mesh Network can provide a significant contribution to the current knowledge base of rural wireless mesh implementations. Specifically we have shown that a locally talent driven solution can be found to meet basic internet needs using mesh technology. Although the mesh network does require considerable attention and care in setup and maintenance, it is a viable current solution for low-bandwidth networks. Simply put, rural indoor to indoor Hybrid

Wireless Mesh Network are a workable solution, but one has to be aware of its limitations under current technology. These technology constraints are a much needed area of current research and it is hoped that the lessons learned from the Macha Network Implementation will serve as a motivation for future research. Unfortunately, test bed solutions produced in laboratories and Universities are far too often not realized in real world rural African environments inundated with unique challenges. Thus there remains a great need for test cases like Macha to be included in the academic research community.

References

1. dd-wrt.com, http://www.dd-wrt.com/site/index
2. Freifunk, http://start.freifunk.net/
3. Human development indices: A statistical update (2008), http://hdr.undp.org
4. Malaria Institute at Macha, http://www.machamalaria.org (accessed 2009)
5. Open-mesh, http://www.open-mesh.com
6. Openwrt: Wireless freedom, http://www.openwrt.org/
7. D.I.Y. Mesh Guide (2007), http://wirelessafrica.meraka.org.za
8. LinkNet Multi-Purpose Co-operative Society Limited (2009), http://www.link.net.zm
9. Backens, J.D., Song, M., Engels, L.: Rural Wireless Mesh Networks in Africa: An Experiential Study. CATA, 128–133 (2009)
10. Johnson, D., Ntlatlapa, N., Aichele, C.: A simple pragmatic approach to mesh routing using BATMAN. In: 2nd IFIP International Symposium on Wireless Communications and Information Technology in Developing Countries, CSIR, Pretoria, South Africa, pp. 6–7 (2008)
11. Johnson, D., Hancke, G.: Comparison of two routing metrics in OLSR on a grid based mesh network. Ad Hoc Networks 7(2), 374–387 (2009)
12. Johnson, D.L., Roux, K.: Building rural wireless networks: Lessons learnt and future directions. In: Proceedings of the 2008 ACM workshop on Wireless networks and systems for developing regions, pp. 17–22. ACM, New York (2008)
13. LinkNet. LinkNet Masterplan: Communications for Rural Zambia (2007), http://link.net.zm/?q=node/30
14. Matthee, K.W., Mweemba, G., Pais, A.V., Van Stam, G., Rijken, M.: Bringing Internet connectivity to rural Zambia using a collaborative approach. In: Proc. 2nd IEEE/ACM ICTD (2007)
15. Pais, A.: eLearning for rural communities (2007), http://www.link.net.zm
16. Surana, S., Patra, R., Nedevschi, S., Ramos, M., Subramanian, L., Ben-David, Y., Brewer, E.: Beyond pilots: keeping rural wireless networks alive. In: NSDI 2008: Proceedings of the 5th USENIX Symposium on Networked Systems Design and Implementation, Berkeley, CA, USA, pp. 119–132. USENIX Association (2008)
17. Van Stam, G.: Case: Sunflower farming. Internet changes Rural Africa (2007), http://www.link.net.zm

e-Justice Implementation at a National Scale: The Ugandan Case

Fredrick Edward Kitoogo[1] and Constantine Bitwayiki[2]

[1] Faculty of Computing and IT, Makerere University, Uganda,
fkitoogo@cit.mak.ac.ug
http://cit.ac.ug/cit/students

[2] Devinovit Associates Limited, Kampala, Uganda

Abstract. The use of information and communications technologies has been identified as one of the means suitable for supplementing the various reforms in convalescing the performance of the justice sector. The Government of Uganda has made strides in the implementation of e-Government to effectively utilize information and communications technologies in governance. The justice players are manifested in a justice, law and order sector which is based on the the Sector Wide Approach whose basic principle is that communication, cooperation and coordination between institutions can greatly add value to service delivery within a sector. Although a subset of e-Government, e-Justice aims at improving service delivery and collaboration between all justice players through the use of ICTs and needs to be spear-headed at a sector level. This work proposes ways of harnessing the existing opportunities and methods to implement e-Justice in Uganda that will culminate into a generic framework that can be applied in similar countries.

Keywords: e-Government, e-Justice, information and communication technologies.

1 Introduction

The improvement of justice delivery world over is becoming a necessity. The use of information and communications technologies has been acknowledged as one of the means improving service delivery in governments and specifically in the justice sector. In Uganda many initiatives have been taken to utilize information and communications technologies in improving delivery of services by Government [1]. Initiatives taken range from those taken by government at the top; such as the creation of Information and Communications Technology Ministry that is at the helm of spear-heading Infromation and Communications Technology (ICT) usage in the country to those taken individually by the different Government Ministries, Departments and Agencies.

The Government of Uganda has moved to formulate an e-Government strategy through an inter-agency team. The e-Government strategy is aimed at guiding the process of implementing e-Government in Uganda [2]. There is also an going

A. Villafiorita, R. Saint-Paul, and A. Zorer (Eds.): AFRICOMM 2009, LNICST 38, pp. 40–49, 2010.

initiative of formulating a National ICT Policy which is led by the Ministry of ICT (MoICT)and the National Planning Authority (NPA)[3].

In the justice sector, several ICT initiatives have been attempted in the different institutions, namely; development of ICT Strategies, ICT Policies, Websites, Intranets, Management Information Systems, and Case Management Systems. All the different innovations are forms of e-Justice and are geared to utilizing ICTs in the improvement of justice delivery [4], [5].

The justice sector broadly entitled the justice, law and order sector (JLOS) includes agencies and institutions concerned with safety, security, and access to justice [6]. The JLOS is specifically is composed of the following institutions: The Ministry of Justice and Constitutional Affairs, Ministry of Internal Affairs, The Judiciary, Uganda Prisons Service, Uganda Police Force, Directorate of Public Prosecutions, The Judicial Service Commission, The Uganda Law Reform Commission, Ministry of Local Government - Local Council Courts, Ministry of Gender, Labour and Social Development - Probation Services.

The Government of Uganda and the donor community have supported the development of a Sector Wide Approach (SWAp) to the justice, law and order sector since 1999. In the SWAp, the JLOS institutions jointly plan and budget in an effort to rationalize and maximize service delivery. It is a basic principle in the SWAp that communication, cooperation and coordination between the JLOS institutions can add value to the activities therein [6]. The sector is further, however, composed of the Judiciary which is an autonomous and independent arm of state whose main function is interpreting laws, adjudicating disputes, and administering and delivering justice to the people of a country. The justice sector, thus, might not be simply another sector for straightforward e-government implementations.

Although, e-Justice is a a subset of e-Government, there is justified need for the justice institutions to move the e-Justice implementation as a sector. The e-Justice implementation at the sector level will the feed into the overall e-Government implementation.

This work examines the Ugandan situation in a relative viewpoint and the work is organized as follows. The first section of the work deals with generic e-Government and e-Justice. The second section focuses on the Ugandan case of ICT implementations towards e-Government and e-Justice examining the situation through a SWOT analysis. The third section proposes a framework for implementation of e-Justice in Uganda emphasizing best practices of technological advances that can improve judicial institutional reforms and enhancing their impacts. The work ends with concluding observations which wrap up the concerns, trends and strategies.

2 e-Justice and e-Government

e-Justice is easily presumed to be a mere subset and section of e-Government implementation, however the justice arena is a rather peculiar area that requires a sector consideration.

e-Justice aims at improving service delivery and collaboration between all justice players through the use of ICT whereas e-Government facilitates online access to various government services including justice, security, agriculture, education, health, etc. e-Government also promotes participation and democracy through public access to information/records in possession of the state or public body, so as to effectively scrutinize and participate in government decisions that affect them [13], [7], [8].

In Uganda [9], e-Justice and Cyber-laws have been identified as a key cross cutting issues that needs to be in place for the successful implementation of e-Government applications in East Africa.

2.1 e-Government

e-Government involves focusing on the use of Information and Communications Technology (ICT) to assist in the transformation of government structures and operations for cooperative and integrated service delivery. More so, e-Government is not just simply putting government forms on-line, creating static organizational websites or posting simple tax schedules on-line, but rather it is the integration of government operations in the delivery of services to her citizenry and the business sector [10] .

e-Government is broadly defined as the use of ICT to promote a more efficient and effective government, facilitates accessibility to government services, allows greater public access to information, and makes government more accountable to citizens. It involves delivering services via the Internet, telephone, electronic media, community centers (self-service or facilitated by others), wireless devices or other communications systems [11].

African countries like Egypt and Mauritius have advanced national e-Government programs with aspects of use of ICT in their judicial systems. Kenya and Rwanda are progressing very well as far as the introduction of e-Government services is concerned [12] .

2.2 e-Justice

The use of information and communications technology in the justice sector has been in constant progress; from the simple access of legal resources via the Internet to the prospect of electronic communication with all parties involved in court business. The use of ICTs not only facilitates the networking at the justice level but also helps the citizens, business operatives and the legal practitioners in their access to justice. Public awareness and culture is also demanding that legal systems be more open and approachable [13]

Although e-Justice may have not yet been totally accepted as a natural language concept, there exist some definitions like; e-Justice is the legal-adjudication-and-enforcement arrangements, gradually absorbing more ICT-services in their operational architectures [14].

e-Justice is generally the use of ICT in the effective and efficient delivery of judicial services. The aim of e-Justice is to make the administration of justice more efficient, effective and less expensive for citizens and all justice players. In a nutshell, e-Justice aims at strengthening the justice system through the the use of ICTs to strengthen the communication and exchange of information amongst the justice players and those seeking justice [15].

Often, also e-Justice refers to the modernization of the administration and delivery of justice through re-engineering work processes by using ICTs [16].

In Africa there are a diversity of judicial systems because of the inheritance of different legal systems due to colonialism [17]. The miscellany in the judicial systems in Africa means a variety of ICT solutions both technically and administratively espoused by the different countries and offers a unique situation in the application of ICTs in the administration of justice. A big challenge lies ahead in benchmarking from the different ICT implementations towards e-Justice.

There are a few targeted full blown implementations of e-Justice in Africa, such as the case of South Africa [18] where the e-Justice programme aims to reform and modernize the administration and delivery of justice through re-engineering work processes by using technologies, and strengthening strategic planning and management capacity, organizational development and human-resource intervention.

3 The Uganda e-Justice and e-Government Case

There have been various passive attempts have been made to towards the implementation of e-Government and e-Justice by the individual institutions.

3.1 ICT Implementations towards e-Government

Amongst one of the biggest underlying implementations towards e-Government is in the telecommunications sectors; today, almost all the districts in the country are covered by the telecommunications infrastructure. To ensure good quality service delivery, more than 80% of all the Public Switching Telephone Network (PSTN) switching systems in the country are digital. Liberalization of the telecom sector has led to its phenomenal growth . There are currently 21 telecommunications operators and slightly over 8 million subscribers. Broadband penetration, ICT usage and provision of basic communications facilities is being promoted by the Uganda Communications Commission (UCC) through the Rural Communications Development Programme (RCDP)[19]. This initiative has covered most of the rural areas considered commercially inviable by incumbent telecommunications operators.

In addition, a National data transmission and e-Government backbone infrastructure (NBI/EGI) is being installed by the Government and expected to be completed by 2010 [2]. The National Data Transmission Backbone is to span through 28 districts while the e-Government infrastructure is to connect all Government Ministries and Departments. All district local governments in the country have websites developed under the Rural Communication Development

Program (RCDP). Public, investment and other business information opportunities are published on the websites. A Government of Uganda web portal to act as a gateway to government services with linkages to the business sector is under development. A National Data Centre to facilitate government wide data storage, usage, sharing and security has been built.

In Uganda, there are already prominent existing ICT implementations towards the actualization of e-Government such as the Integrated Personnel and Payroll System, Integrated Financial Management System and e-Health.

3.2 ICT Implementations towards e-Justice

In Uganda, tremendous resources have been invested in ICT projects in the different justice sector institutions to improve the efficiency and effectiveness of the justice system. The different projects have targeted criminal, civil and administrative operations within the different justice institutions. This section broadly describes some of the individual institutional initiatives.

The Judiciary through donor support has been at the forefront of utilization of ICT in the improvement of justice delivery through various projects such as the Court Case Administration System (CCAS) which is a case management system that assists in recording all details pertaining to a case (file), tracking files, cause listing, generation of statistics and monitoring performance. The Judiciary also initiated the use of a Court Recording and Transcription System which is geared to quickening the preparation of court proceedings and judgments. A Management Information System (MIS) has also been developed for the Judiciary to store and report on management information. On top of all other implementations are the Intranet and Website which are geared to increasing transparency, collaboration and communication. Lastly, an electronic document management system (EDMS) is in the process of being deployed to streamline the life-cycle of document handling. All the systems are working in a networked environment at individual stations, some of which are connected via a Wide Area Network (WAN)[4].

The Directorate of Public Prosecutions through donor support has also attempted to utilize ICTs by amongst others networking some major stations and deploying a case management system referred to as PROCAM whose main aim was to support the timely administration and delivery of services by the Directorate to the Public. The system was also specifically targeted to monitor case files and monitor performance of the other sector institutions (Judiciary and Police)[5].

The Police until of recent had not clearly utilized much ICT, save for the TETRA digital trunk radio communications system for enabling efficient communication between Ugandas security agencies [20]. The Uganda Police enthusiastically made strides towards integrating ICTs in its service delivery by signing a memorandum of understanding with Makerere University (FCIT) in which the two parties shall be responsible for the design, development and implementation of appropriate electronic information and communication solutions/applications and the selection of the equipment to be used based on compatibility with the existing Government standards and policies [21].

The Uganda Prisons has not embraced concrete ICT Systems, it is currently using a few computer equipment for word processing and worksheets to store some information.

3.3 SWOT Analysis

In this section, a critical strengths, weaknesses, Oppportunitites and Threats analysis has been conducted basing on practical experience and some inspirations in [13]

1. **Strengths**
   - The different justice institutions have already started ICT implementations towards e-Justice at the institutional level.
2. **Weaknesses**
   - Most ICT initiatives are purely focused on the computerization of activities not necessarily interconnected with the larger judicial reform agenda. The administration mainly concentrates on procurement of hardware (computers) and not the systems that will really impact on the Judicial reform
   - In justice sector institutions, there are deficient organizational arrangements for the planning and implementation of ICT investments. There is also a lack of planning mechanisms, poor arrangements for discharging responsibilities, a lack of opportunities for systematic learning by justice sector staff.
   - Lack of knowledge of senior policy makers on the importance of ICT and their commitment to modernize. Benefits and opportunities available with ICT to improve business processes and core judicial operations are not well articulated. Efforts to improve access to justice, citizen participation and communications that can be leveraged through the introduction of technologies, have generally not been targeted to appropriate levels of decision makers. Too many of the initiatives are handled at low levels that have functional rather than decision-making authority and clout. This has at times resulted in funding cut-offs and shelved projects.
   - There is Lack of donor coordination. Projects in in the different justice institutions have failed to get coordinated due to failures to integrate aid from different sources, resulting in disparate equipment and software specifications, and business processes that cannot collaborate.
   - Lack of sufficient institutional stakeholder involvement and training which undermines change. Another flaw has been inadequate consultation with the concerned stakeholders, especially on their perceptions of, and readiness to implement ICT induced changes. As ICT programs often result in new work methods and behavior, the participation and education of employees and users is fundamental. Programs that overlook factors of resistance to change almost invariably fail sooner or later.

3. **Opportunities**
   - There are some existing e-justice solutions with some vendors and they are compatible with the already implemented e-Government systems in government (Min. of Finance Integrated Financial Management System, Min. of Public Service Integrated Personnel and Payroll System and Min of Local Government - LOGICS). The solutions can be implemented at a subsidized cost if they utilize the already existing infrastructure.
   - The existence of the National Data Transmission Backbone Infrastructure (NBI) can be used to interconnect the different justice players as well as the public.
   - Donor funding as has been in the past, the advantage now is that the funding is at now supported through the JLOS (Sector-wide Approach)
4. **Threats**
   - The main threat is the determination of who should be the lead institution in the implementation of the integrated initiative.
   - The different justice institutions already have isolated islands of ICT implementations which might be fragmented, overlapping and unrelated. There is a challenge of integrating the different systems. There could be two directions; one is to implement an entirely new integrated system from scratch and another would be integrate the already existing systems.
   - There is a threat of staff within the justice institutions failing to reform their work habits towards the support of e-Justice implementation

It is evident that on one side, there are a good number of ICT projects initiated, but, on the other side, the biggest problem is that the realizations of the original project goals have not been achieved to the entirety.

The ICT projects/implementations in the different institutions have been done independently without a common framework for integration, implying that there is no effective communication for information sharing, collaboration across and within the complex boundaries.

4 The e-Justice Solution and Framework

The biggest concern in the sector (JLOS) is the perceived dwindling speed and quality of justice (all players in the sector have a role to play) in the country; the root causes are insufficient vertical and horizontal linkages [6] and inability to efficiently collaborate and share information within the sector.

The different ICT implementations, e.g. CCAS and PROCAM had an objective of integrating information from other justice institutions and this was not realized. This concern strengthens the need for e-Justice.

4.1 The e-Justice Solution

The gaps in the current e-Justice attempts can be filled by having a fully blown e-Justice system which shall embrace the following aspects in order to offer a total solution to the ineffectiveness and inefficiency in the delivery of justice:

1. Integrated Justice System; This should offer a common framework for the information exchange between the different sector players (Judiciary, Police, DPP, Prisons, Min of Justice, etc.).
2. Through e-Justice, Electronic Filing should be possible at all the institutions; i.g the litigants through advocates should be able to file cases electronically, likewise the police should be able to file with the DPP electronically and the Judiciary should be able to relay conviction information to the Uganda prisons electronically. Furthermore, it would be possible to alert Prisons Authorities about suspects who automatically qualify for bail.
3. Through e-Justice it should be possible track cases right from the police through to prison stages and within the different stages
4. Through the implementation of e-Justice, incidences of lost case files will be minimized in all institutional categories
5. Through e-Justice it is possible to monitor performance and identify bottlenecks within the entire justice system (with the ability to make trigger reports and alarms when time-lines are violated)
6. Through e-Justice it is possible to produce integrated statistics that are representative of the all the justice sector players (e.g. Defilement cases with details of victims this integrates both Judiciary and Police/DPP information).

4.2 Proposed Framework of Implementing e-Justice

The implementation of e-Justice is not a fully exploited area and thus does not have a straightforward methodology that can be adopted largely because the area is still novel, existing differences in justice systems, maintenance of the need for the independence of the Judiciary.

Basing on some attempts to e-Justice earlier referred to in the previous sections, the following is the preferred framework for the implementation of e-Justice in justice systems similar to that of Uganda. The proposed judicial portal is also shown in Figure 1:

1. The e-Justice implementation should be **championed by the Ministry of Justice** as has been the case for other justice reform policies and strategies [22]
2. Creation of an **e-Justice Task force/Steering Committee** of the different players to drive the implementation
3. Creation of an **e-justice strategy and e-Justice Policy** to guide the implementation and adherenace
4. **Inventory all the existing institutional ICT initiatives and identify existing manual synergies** that requires integration and information sharing
5. Determine all the major **e-Justice arenas** with a view of creating a **common Portal** that will facilitate e-Justice and will be characterized by the following functionality:
   - Electronic Judicial Procedures and Law Reporting

   - Electronic filing, Document Scanning and Management
   - Interconnection of all judicial Records from all JLOS players
   - Creation/Access to various Databases (Advocates, Bailiffs, Court Stations)
   - Bulletins: exchange of documents and information within and between justice institutions and the public
   - Video Conferencing, Proceedings Recording and Transcription
   - Lawyers and Citizens Portal
   - Data mining and real time management of judiciary in an electronic environment
6. **Awareness Campaigns** of e-Justice
7. Consider ways of **integration of the already existing individual institutional initiatives into the e-Justice Framework**
8. **Legal issues and challenges through introduction of e-justice** (apart from Computer Crime, Electronic Transactions and Digital Signatures)

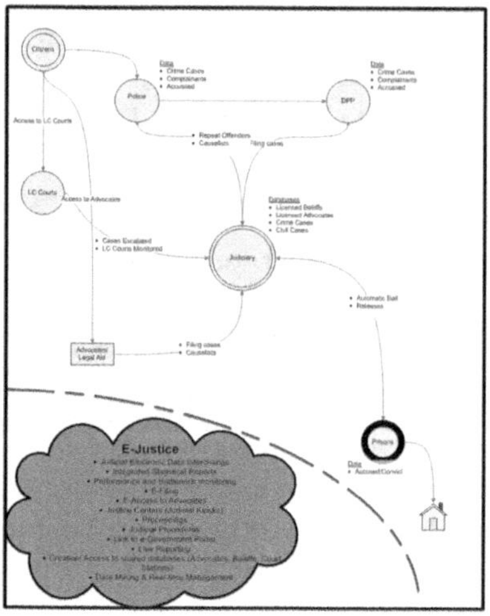

Fig. 1. e-Justice-Portal (Access by the Public and Institutions to the Justice Systems)

5 Conclusion

There is still very limited information in circulation about the use of ICT in the administration of justice. This is despicable because common challenges faced to which solutions have been modeled can not be shared. This study of the Ugandan case could trigger more studies and contribute significantly to the sharing of experiences towards the implementation of e-Justice that will culminate in a cohesive framework.

It should also be emphasized that the administration of justice is still treated as a island and lagging behine in the e-Government implementations. It is about the right time that the justice sector is made one of the top priorities for e-Government projects in Uganda and other LDCs.

References

1. The National ICT Master Plan and e-Government feasibility study for Uganda (2006)
2. Uganda e-Government Strategic Framework Final Draft, National Planning Authority (2007)
3. Mulira, H.M.: Ministerial Policy Statement. Financial Year 2007/2008 (2007)
4. The Ugandan Judiciary Website, http://www.judicature.go.ug
5. The Ugandan Directorate of Public Prosecution Website, http://www.dpp.go.ug
6. Edroma, E.B.: Sector Wide Approach in Justice Law and Order: The Uganda Experience. In: Annual Conference on Fusion of Legal Systems and Concepts in Africa, September 4-7 (2005)
7. Bozeman, B., Bretschneider, S.: Public Management Information Systems: Theory and Prescription. Public Administration Review 46(Special issue) (1986)
8. Bretschneider, S.: Management Information Systems in Public and Private Organizations: an Empirical Test. Public Administration Review 50(5) (1990)
9. EAC- Cyber Laws, E-justice and E-security Stakeholders Consultative Workshop, http://www.a-2-a.net/a-2-a.net/index.php%3FnewsID=45.html
10. Maddalena, S.: The Implementation of ICT in Public Sector Organisations. Analysing Selection Criteria for e-Government Projects (2004)
11. The Working Group on e-Government in the Developing World.: Roadmap for e-Government in the Developing World: 10 Questions e-Government Leaders Should Ask Themselves. Los Angeles: Pacific Council on International Policy (2002)
12. Rorissa, A., Demissie, D.: The State of the Art of E-Government Services in Africa: An Analysis of Relevant Websites (2009)
13. Malik, W.H.: E-Justice: Towards a Strategic Use of ICT in Judicial Reform (2002)
14. Schmidt, A.: E-Justice: No Ground for Optimism (2009)
15. Politis, D., Papasteriadou, N. (eds.): Recent advances on court computerization and legal databases – first steps towards e-justice. Ant. N. Sakkoulas, Athens (2003)
16. UNDP: eGovernance-Africa, http://ictd.undp.org/africaegov/en/menu_info.php?table=eg_menu6
17. Joireman, S.F.: Inherited legal systems and effective rule of law: Africa and the colonial legacy. The Journal of Modern African Studies 39(4), 571–596 (2002)
18. South African Government Information, Integrated Justice System, IJS (2009), http://www.info.gov.za/aboutgovt/justice/system.htm#ejustice
19. Tusubira, F.F., Kaggwa-Sewankambo, I., Kyeyune, A., Ndiwalana, A.: Uganda Telecommunications Sector Performance Reviews (2007)
20. Motorola's TETRA Digital Communications System Uganda Police Force Deploys, http://itvoir.com/portal/resources/Mobile-Search-Engine/Motorola-s-TETRA-Digital-Communications-System-Uganda-Police-Force-Deploys.asp
21. Collaboration of FCIT with the Uganda Police Forc, http://www.cit.ac.ug/cit/project_details.php?item=59
22. Edroma, E.B.: Aid Effectiveness and Civil Society: Experiences from the Justice Law and Order Sector of Uganda. Seminar on Aid: The Paris Declaration and its Implementation (2007)

Supporting Public Administration with an Integrated BPR Environment

Aaron Ciaghi[1], Adolfo Villafiorita[1], Komminist Weldemariam[1,2], Andrea Mattioli[1], and Quoc-Sang Phan[1,2]

[1] Fondazione Bruno Kessler (fbk-irst), Italy
via Sommarive 14, I-38050 Trento, Italy
{ciaghi,adolfo,sisai,amattioli,phan}@fbk.eu

[2] Department of Information Engineering and Computer Science,
University of Trento, via Sommarive 18, I-38050 Trento, Italy
{weldemar@disi,quocsang.phan@studenti}.unitn.it

Abstract. The definition or redesign of Public Administration (PA) procedures is particularly challenging. This is, for example, due to the requirement of cooperation of different organizational units and actors, different laws and procedures for the production of several artifacts, and maintaining traceability while integrating processes with new laws.

We are interested in business process modeling and re-engineering (BPR) for PA, where ICT can play a pivotal role by, e.g., improving communication among law-makers and process analysts. With regard to this previously we developed a tool called VLPM[1]. The tool is designed to provide assistance in BPR for PA, which allows traceability between laws and processes. In this paper, we discuss the extension of the tool and of its methodology to support an integrated environment that can be used for better law and process re-design by performing formal analysis on the processes. We discuss its system components and provide a working example taken from the Italian Immigration law, as a proof of concept.

1 Introduction

One of the most recent trends undertaken by the ICT community in the support of public administration (PA) is based on the use of business process modeling (BPR) techniques [1,2,3]. More specifically, the use of modeling languages to graphically represent PA procedures as business processes in order to redesign such procedures is becoming a widespread practice. For instance, the use of BPR for better government has been discussed earlier by the US federal government and the US Department of Defense [4]. Its specific uses for public services such as in taxation and in healthcare, widely discussed, e.g., in [5,6,7,8]. This approach is helpful not only in a process redesign scenario but also in situations where legal procedures are neither well-documented or clearly-defined nor presented at all (e.g., think of the land management in some developing countries).

[1] Visual Law Process Modeler: http://ed.fbk.eu/vlpm/

A. Villafiorita, R. Saint-Paul, and A. Zorer (Eds.): AFRICOMM 2009, LNICST 38, pp. 50–59, 2010.

Various works that describe how to use modeling languages and formal methods for modeling, specifying and analyzing business processes and workflows have been presented in, e.g., [9,10]. However, little is usually said on the attempt to model laws and procedures, and perform formal analysis in favor of the PA processes. To tackle this, in [11] we presented a tool called VLPM. The tool uses a subset of UML diagrams guided by strictly defined methodology in order to represent the laws and procedures as business process models, which are organized as static and dynamic process views and support their manual analysis. It also generates a well-formed documentation (e.g., in HTML or PDF).

In this paper, we discuss the roadmap for VLPM and a set of first extensions aimed at providing a new set of functions for analyzing, while, at the same time, improving interaction, usability, and portability.

2 Challenges of ICT-Supported PA

Procedures in PA are typically encoded in formal documents and laws. In what follows we discuss the main challenges we experienced in representing, modeling, and analyzing legal documents as (business) process. These challenges, in fact, represent a set of user requirements for the development of VLPM$^+$.

1. **Interpretation.** In several countries information related to legal regulations are spread across laws and procedures. This can allow different actors to interpret the same concept encoded in the same law or procedure differently. As a result, this arises issues related to *inconsistencies*, when the definition of one law conflicts with other law(s). For instance, an Italian old but still valid royal charter states t hat only who is Italian or European citizen can be employed in public transportation services. However, another law promulgated in 1998 states that any resident in Italy can be employed in the public service.
2. **Methodology and Tools.** Using modeling tools (such as, UML Activity Diagrams [12], BPML [13]) for creating workflow (or activity) diagrams has different advantages. For example, the mapping and visualization of the processes help the stakeholders to easily communicate and understand the processes. However, as pointed out also in [2], customizations are needed to make the representation clear and usable.
3. **Change Management Support.** When process modeling is used with the goal of re-engineering processes, an important aspect is guaranteeing "synchronization" between the model representation and the laws, so that any change to the process can be reflected in an equivalent amendment to the law and the other way round.

Besides the above challenges we also mention some of requirements for modeling e-Government processes given in [2]:

1. process models must contain the relevant subjects, objects, activities, events and constraints of administrative processes that make up a transaction;

2. e-Government process models should be standardized so that they can be synchronized and put together with other such processes to form a one-stop solution for their end users;
3. the resulting models shall be able to show the restrictions for re-engineering that are set by the legal framework or other public regulations;
4. method and notation must not be too complex since administrative executives are usually not familiar with modeling languages.

3 Framework for Supporting PA

VLPM is a tool, freely available tool and built as a Visual-Paradigm plug-in, designed to support process modeling and re-engineering for the public administration. It provides a set of functions to synchronize models and XML representation of laws. It is worth mentioning that as of the currently version the tool only supports the Italian laws. We are working to make the tool more flexible and more functional in various areas, among which we mention support for different XML representation of laws (which are used by VLPM for linking process and laws); more flexibility in deployment (e.g. by allowing integration with freely available UML tools); integration with formal analysis techniques (for simulation and verification, e.g., [14].

The resulting tool, VLPM^{+}, will provide the following functions:

1. *Provide static view of processes.* It consists of of a set of modeling methodology and functions to help in identifying, representing, and modeling laws and procedures as business processes. (Currently provided by VLPM.)
2. *Change Management and Traceability of the Process.* Maintaining law-model traceability while changing the model can allow to automatically identify which parts of the law should be amended by tracing back to the parts of the law that originally defined the modified processes. Performing re-engineering on some process might also require to update the model, which in turn must ensure traceability between laws and new processes. (Partly provided by VLPM.)
3. *Generate Documentation.* To improve the information sharing and further communication among the different organizational units as well as actors VLPM generate a well-formed documentation. (Currently provided by VLPM).
4. *Formal Analysis of the Model.* Here, our aim is to support analysis of the processes with formal methods (such as, model checking and simulation). In this way we can formally analyze laws and procedures, define a boundary to perform procedural security analysis, and list suggestions and identify critical points. (New function of VLPM^{+}).
5. *Customization and Installation Options.* VLPM is based on two standards, the Italian XML representation of laws and the UML. VLPM+ will support customization of the XML standard to support schema adopted by other nations and allow for the integration of UML tools providing standard connection "ports" to the UML (e.g., XMI).

4 System Description

4.1 Intermediate Representation of Model Elements

In order to have a representation of processes flexible enough to represent the portability and usability scenarios described above and support formal analysis, we developed the metamodel shown in Figure 1. The core modeling elements are *process, actor, asset,* and *relationships.*

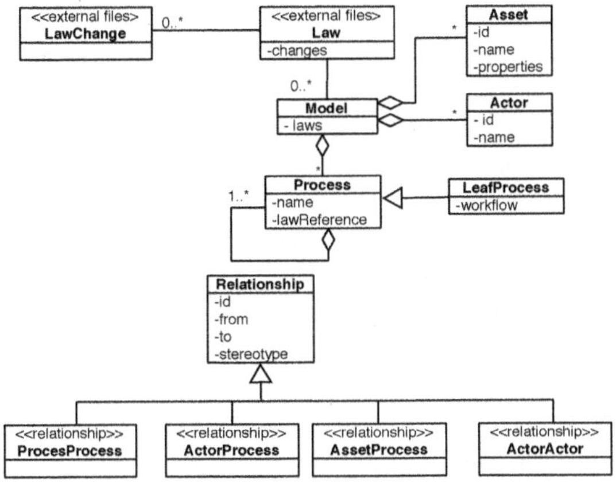

Fig. 1. Modeling Elements' Metamodel

A *process* is realized as an observable activity executed by one or more *actors*, which might be person, components, technical systems of combinations thereof. In particular, we use the definition of process as described in our UML modeling methodology [11] where processes are hierarchically organized. Each process is associated to law elements that define and regulate it. Leaf processes in the hierarchy contain the actual specification of processes as a sequence of activities —in our methodology they contain activity diagrams, written in a specific language that can be translated to UML or to asset flows on which formal analysis using the state of the art techniques can subsequently be performed.

An *actor* is responsible for a specific process or asset. Actors can be extracted from the text of the law or can be defined manually. Currently, our model identifies them by means of an unambiguous identifier (extracted from the XML file containing the law information) and a name. However, this could easily be extended in order to add more features, for instance, stereotypes.

Assets are what we focus on when performing formal analysis of processes and, in particular, security assessments. In the same way as actors, they can be either extracted from the law or defined manually. Assets are characterized by a feature which comprises of a set of properties, value and location. A particular instance of an asset feature defines its state. Asset flows describe the evolution of assets, i.e., possible sequences of states through which assets can proceed during its lifetime as a result of reacting to discrete activities performed on the asset feature (i.e., the value, location, and properties) and possibly other conditions meet. In our model, we store the initial states of assets and we use our notation to define the changes that the assets undergo.

Relationships are defined separately from the objects of the model. We use a generic relationship element to create specific sub-classes of relationships. *Actor-Actor* relationships have different properties from *Actor-Process* relationships (e.g., the allowed stereotypes) and from *Process-Process* relationships. To associate a process with its executing actors (i.e., *Actor-Process* relationship), we use the concept of *roles*. A role has a name $\in R$, where R is the set of role identifiers. The use of an abstract relationship object allows us to create as many types of relationship as we need, with the only requirement of defining also a suitable translation of each relationship to UML. We also explicitly support the *Asset-Process* relationships that define the semantics for the asset flows. In addition, the modeling borrows and extends some well-known formalisms from the RACIV responsibility matrix, and from the CRUD matrix, to support the different relationships discussed above.

The model represents the static information of the business processes, while the dynamic properties (namely, asset transformation functions) are defined in a specific notation. The model is associated to the laws that regulate its business processes to allow the association of a single process with relevant law parts that define them. Notice that the law is not included in the model. For our case studies, we used examples from the Italian law system retrieved using the *Normeinrete* [15,16] project and its XML format. Although our metamodel is designed to support XML format for laws representation, it can be easily extended to support other formats.

4.2 System Components

We devised a 3-tier architecture based on a representation of the model which is independent from the tools used to visualize it and to perform formal analysis. In particular, the main system components are (see Figure 2):

1. **Data:** This contains the actual data on which the system operates as well as the visualization of models. In particular, it is responsible for comprising the process model (i.e., in XML model), XML representation of laws associated with processes in the model, UML modeling tool, and formal specifications' data (the *Intermediate Model*).
2. **Services:** Provide the core functionalities of the tool and contain the following components:
   - **Change Manager.** It provides all the functions to modify the model, import external modifications (e.g., amendments to the law regulating the processes being modeled) and analyze the impact of changes in the model to the law.
   - **Translation.** This is a class of components used to convert one form of model representation into other representations – namely, printable

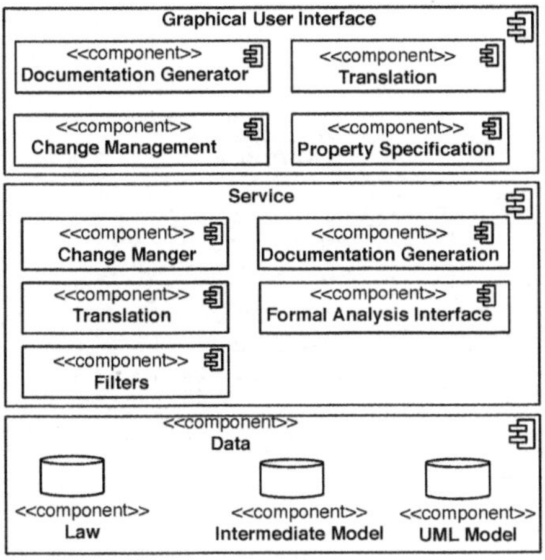

Fig. 2. The proposed VLPM$^+$ System's Reference Architecture

documentation and formal models – as well as extract procedures from the law and convert the changes in the model to possible changes to the law.

- **Documentation Generation.** It is responsible for generating human readable documentation of the model or of a subset of it.
- **Formal Analysis Interface.** It provides an interface to the formal analysis environment. This works together with a component that translates the workflow (in the form of activity diagrams) in the model to asset flows and subsequently to, e.g., NuSMV modules or other target formal tool. This part of the system also provides a service to assign feature values (e.g., asset properties) to the assets involved and to specify the security requirements that must be checked against the process model and asset flows. We do so by using the *property specification* GUI.

3. **Graphical User Interfaces.** They facilitate user interaction with the system. Since laws and processes are specified in natural language, some activities in the modeling workflow require some user intervention, e.g., in order to decide how to translate specific parts of a law in an ambiguous way, etc. More specifically, using respective interfaces the user is allowed to specify which subset should pass to the corresponding translator component (*Translation*), to specify critical requirements for formal analysis (*Property Specification*), to provide changes to the model based on the (formal) analysis report (*Change Management*), etc. Each of these components could pass through respective *filter component* – which allows the user to filter a complex model to produce a relevant information – before the subsequent steps.

5 Case Study

We used the Italian Immigration law as a case study for the preliminary analysis of the use cases of our integrated platform. Specifically, we analyzed the entrance

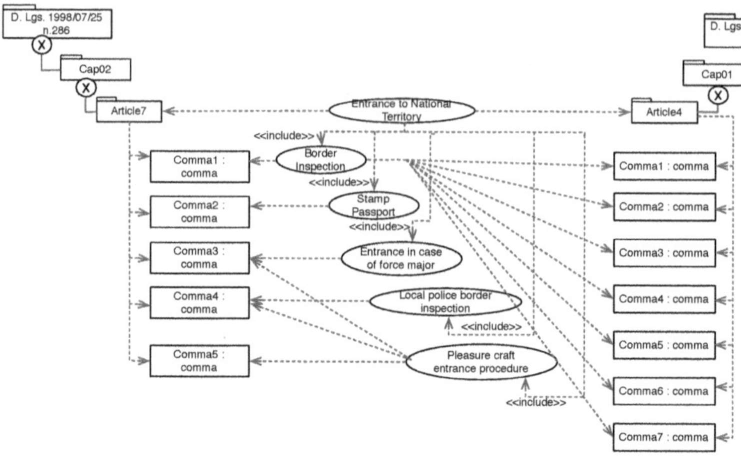

Fig. 3. Process Tree: Entrance into Italian National Territory

procedures at the Italian border and the required documents as defined in the 286th legislative decree of July, 25 1998 on "Consolidated Act of Provisions concerning immigration and the condition of third country nationals" and in the 394th presidential decree of August, 31 1999 (with all their changes until now). We considered the latter as the *primary law*, from which the process structure was extracted, and the former as an *additional law*, from which we derived extra dependencies.

We started applying our modeling methodology, which in this paper is simpler than the one presented in [11], in order to obtain the process decomposition tree shown in Figure 3. The figure highlights the *many-to-many* relationship among processes and the law paragraphs they are derived from or constrained by, but excludes actors which are involved in their realization. The two laws also provide information related to the order of the processes and related to the modification of assets (e.g., the *property* of the `Passport` was *"NotStamped"* and became *"Stamped & Inspected"*). See an example in Figure 4, which uses an activity diagram to refine the *"Border Inspection"* process.

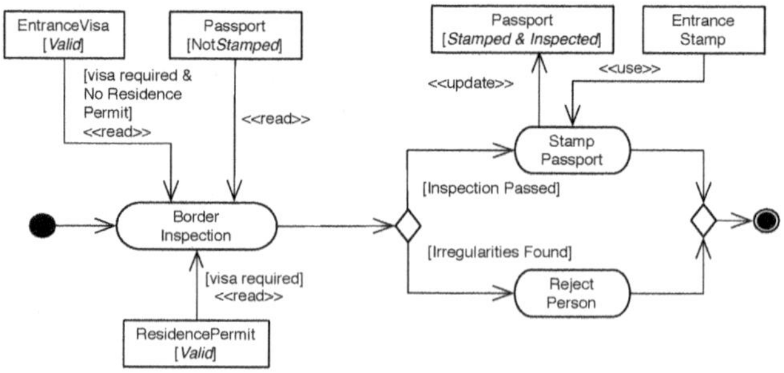

Fig. 4. Border Inspection.

Activity diagrams are strong as modeling means but lacks simulation and verification capabilities [9,10]. As a proof of concept, we manually formalized the diagram depicted in Figure 4 using Algebraic Petri Nets [17], an intermediate format composed of Petri Nets and abstract algebraic data types. Model checker like NuSMV [18] then can be used to perform formal verification and simulation.

The detail how we intend to perform the formalization, translation, verification and activities related to change management is not in the scope of this paper and thus we skip.

6 Related Work

In order to univocally identify laws and their elements, *NormeInRete* uses a URN (Uniform Resource Name) based system [15,19]. The URNs are defined as a combination of elements according to a specific grammar. The basic elements are: name of the promulgating authority, type of norm, date, number and, when needed, a set of more detailed specifications [15]. The authors in [20] presented xmlLeges application, an open source application suite for legal drafting.

The advantages and difficulties related to the (re-)engineering of public services are discussed in [1,2,3,6]. In [5,8,7], the authors particularly discussed the support of ICT for public *healthcare* services by identifying different levels of process support and distinguish between generic process patterns, as well as the level of automation. These approaches, however, lack the supporting tools and their corresponding precise methodology to perform the modeling (in some cases, to perform the analysis) of such processes. !

In [21] the authors propose a UML-based approach to define, verify, and validate organizational processes. More specifically, their modeling and verification are from the point of software process improvement through the CMMI framework (Capability Maturity Model Integration). The author in [22] discussed challenges and opportunities of using simulation techniques to reduce the risks and increase the chance for success of business process re-engineering. Clearly, these approaches are different from us in the sense that they did not particularly face the challenges of the public administration processes.

The importance of modeling in the legal framework and documenting the knowledge about the legal constraints within the process model itself is stated in [2,23]. The authors propose an approach based on Event-driven process chains and suggest how to translate law paragraphs into process models using the Semantic Process Language (SPL). In [24] authors establish the basic need for formal techniques in electronic governance. The authors in [25] also discussed a pattern-based evaluation of UML 2.0 Activity diagrams for workflow modeling. These approaches can be refined and used in order to strength our approach.

7 Conclusion and Future Work

The definition of strict constraints for the structure of a law facilitates its readability and editing, but — in the case of laws definition procedures — the use of visual representations and their formal verification can take this even further. The modeling method itself must not be too complex since administrative executives are usually not familiar with modeling languages.

Although there are still some points need to further refine and develop, in this paper we discuss why it is difficult to adequately support PA processes by ICT systems and which challenges exist in this context. We proposed an integrated environment to overcome some of the mentioned challenges. We are currently implementing the various components discussed in this paper in order to integrate them with the current version of VLPM. In the future, we would like also to support the integration of PA processes on different levels through free simulation. We are also looking for case studies to evaluate our framework in a larger scope.

References

1. David, G., Wastell, P., White, P.: A Methodology for Business Process Redesign: Experiences and Issues. Journal of Strategic Information Systems 3, 23–40 (1994)
2. Alpar, P., Olbrich, S.: Legal Requirements and Modelling of Processes in e-Government. Electronic Journal of e-Government 3 (2005)
3. Xenakis, A., Macintosh, A.: Using Business Process Re-engineering (BPR) for the Effective Administration of Electronic Voting. The Electronic Journal of e-Government 3(2) (2005)
4. U.S.A. National Performance Review. Executive Summary — Creating a Government that Works Better and Costs Less (1993)
5. Willcocks, L., Currie, W., Jackson, S.: Radical Re-Engineering and Information Systems: Evidence from UK Public Services. In: Fifth European Conference in Information Systems, Cork (1997)
6. Thaens, M., Bekkers, V., van Duivenboden, H.: Business Process Redesign and Public Administration: a Perfect Match? In: Taylor, J.A., Snellen, I.T.M., Zuurmond, A. (eds.) Beyond BPR in Public Administration: An Institutional Transformation in an Information Age, pp. 15–36. IOS Press, Amsterdam (1997)
7. Greco, G., Guzzo, A., Pontieri, L.: Mining Hierarchies of Models: From Abstract Views to Concrete Specifications. In: van der Aalst, W.M.P., Benatallah, B., Casati, F., Curbera, F. (eds.) BPM 2005. LNCS, vol. 3649, pp. 32–47. Springer, Heidelberg (2005)
8. Lenz, R., Reichert, M.: IT Support for Healthcare Processes. In: van der Aalst, W.M.P., Benatallah, B., Casati, F., Curbera, F. (eds.) BPM 2005. LNCS, vol. 3649, pp. 354–363. Springer, Heidelberg (2005)
9. Russell, N., van der Aalst, W.M.P., ter Hofstede, A.H.M., Wohed, P.: On the Suitability of UML 2.0 Activity Diagrams for Business Process Modelling. In: Third Asia-Pacific Conference on Conceptual Modelling (APCCM 2006), vol. 53 (2006)
10. Eshuis, R.: Symbolic Model Checking of UML Activity Diagrams. ACM Trans. Softw. Eng. Methodol. 15(1), 1–38 (2006)
11. Ciaghi, A., Villafiorita, A., Mattioli, A.: VLPM: A Tool to Support BPR in Public Administration. In: ICDS, pp. 289–293. IEEE Computer Society, Los Alamitos (2009)
12. Object Managment Group. The Unified Modeling Language (UML2.0) Superstructure Specification. Technical report (2004)

13. Object Managment Group. Business Process Modeling Notation (BPMN). Technical report (2009)
14. Weldemariam, K., Villafiorita, A.: Formal Procedural Security Modeling and Analysis. In: CRiSIS 2008: Third International Conference on Risks and Security of Internet and Systems, Washington, DC, USA, pp. 249–254. IEEE, Los Alamitos (2008)
15. Lupo, C.: NormeinRete: a Federative Approach to On-line Legislation Access. In: International Conference Parliaments' Information Management in Africa: Challenges and Opportunities of ICTs to Strengthen Democracy and Parliamentary Governance, Nairobi, Kenya (2005)
16. Lupo, C.: Formato per la rappresentazione elettronica dei provvedimenti normativi tramite il linguaggio di marcatura XML. Allegato tecnico alla Circolare 22 aprile 2002, n. AIPA/CR/40 (2002)
17. Reisig, W.: Petri Nets and Algebraic Specifications. Theor. Comput. Sci. 80(1), 1–34 (1991)
18. Bertoli, P., Cimatti, A., Pistore, M., Roveri, M., Traverso, P.: NuSMV 2: An Open Source Tool for Symbolic Model Checking. In: Brinksma, E., Larsen, K.G. (eds.) CAV 2002. LNCS, vol. 2404, p. 359. Springer, Heidelberg (2002)
19. de Oliveira Lima, J.A., Palmirani, M., Vitali, F.: 'HTTP" or 'urn' URIs for legal resources? How about both? In: Jurix 2007 Workshop on Legislative XML (2007)
20. Agnoloni, T., Francesconi, E., Spinosa, P.: XMLegesEditor: an OpenSource Visual XML Editor for supporting Legal National Standards. In: V Legislative XML Workshop, pp. 239–251 (2007)
21. Hsueha, N.-L., Shen, W.-H., Yanga, Z.-W., Yanga, D.-L.: Applying UML and software simulation for process definition, verification, and validation. Information and Software Technology 50, 897–911 (2008)
22. Hlupic, V.: Business Process Modelling Using Discrete Event Simulation: Potential Benefits And Obstacles For Wider Use. International Journal of Simulation: Systems, Science and Technology 4, 62–67 (2003)
23. Olbrich, S., Simon, C.: Process Modelling towards e-Government – Visualisation and Semantic Modelling of Legal Regulations as Executable Process Sets. Electronic Journal of e-Government 6 (2008)
24. Davies, J., Janowski, T., Ojo, A.K., Shukla, A.: Technological foundations of electronic governance. In: ICEGOV, pp. 5–11 (2007)
25. Russell, N., van der Aalst, W.M.P., ter Hofstede, A.H.M., Wohed, P.: On the Suitability of UML 2.0 Activity Diagrams for Business Process Modelling. In: Third Asia-Pacific Conference on Conceptual Modelling (APCCM 2006), vol. 53 (2006)

SAMBA Project Experiences

Christian Fuhrhop[1], Raju Vaidya[1], Oscar Mayora[2], and Elizabeth Furtado[3]

[1] Fraunhofer FOKUS, Kaiserin-Augusta-Allee 31, 10589 Berlin, Germany
christian.fuhrhop@fokus.fraunhofer.de,
raju.vaidya@fokus.fraunhofer.de

[2] CREATE-NET, Via alla Cascata 56/D Povo, 38123 Trento, Italy
oscar.mayora@create-net.org

[3] University of Fortaleza, Avenida Washington Soares 1321, Fortaleza, Brazil
elizabet@unifor.br

Abstract. The purpose of the SAMBA project, running from January 2007 to February 2009, was to create a framework for allowing local communities and citizens (including low income population) to access community-oriented content and services by means of iDTV channels, specifically MHP over DVB-T. This paper summarises the project and the experiences gained from it.

Keywords: iDTV, MHP, DVB-T, Brazil, user generated content, Power Line.

1 Introduction

The aim of the SAMBA[1] project was to create a framework that allowed local communities and citizens (including low income population) in Brazil to access Internet-like services, specifically to access community-oriented content and services by means of interactive digital television (iDTV) channels.

The SAMBA project was in part funded by the Information Society Technologies (IST) programme of the European Commission[2] and consisted of partners from Brazil, Italy, Germany and Finland.

Technically, the SAMBA project was based on MHP (Multimedia Home Platform) as the presentation technology, DVB-T (Digital Video Broadcasting Terrestrial) as the broadcast technology and power line for the return channel.

2 Initial Situation

2.1 Location

The testbed for the SAMBA project was in Barreirinhas, a small town in Brazil with about 50000 inhabitants. The city has a number of atypical features, making

[1] System for Advanced interactive digital television and Mobile services in BrAzil.

[2] European Community's Sixth Framework Programme - IST-045403.

A. Villafiorita, R. Saint-Paul, and A. Zorer (Eds.): AFRICOMM 2009, LNICST 38, pp. 60–69, 2010.

it an interesting location for testbeds. Barreirinhas is located in Maranhão, one of the poorest and least developed states in Brazil (26th of 27 states in gross domestic product), with an average annual income of less than 2000 Euro. The city is relatively isolated, with the next city, São Luís, about 250 km away. While the connecting road infrastructure is good, due to a recently built, well maintained road, traffic is sparse and consists mainly of goods and a few buses per day to São Luís.

Due to its location close to Lençóis Maranhenses National Park, tourism is an important source of revenue, even though most of the tourists are individual travellers, usually only staying for a day or two, and the total number of tourists is small, due to the lack of other nearby attractions.

Barreirinhas is a fairly compact city, allowing the deployment of range-limited technologies like DVB-T, Power Line Communication (PLC) or WiMAX while still reaching a reasonable number of households, making it a popular environment for testing new technologies.

2.2 Technology Background

At the time the SAMBA project was planned, no decision had been taken which digital terrestrial television system would be used in Brazil (with ATSC, DVB-T and ISDB-T as possible alternatives), so part of the purpose of the SAMBA project was to demonstrate the capabilities of DVB-T and the MHP middleware.

About half a year into the project, the decision was made in Brazil to use SBTVD (a variant of the Japanese ISDB-T system) as the terrestrial digital TV system, with a new development, Ginga, as the middleware.

Due to the decision in favour of SBTVD, showcasing and promoting DVB-T became less relevant in SAMBA and the project shifted more towards the implementation and provision of services. Since Ginga, specifically the Ginga-J subsystem, supported GEM (Globally Executeable MHP), MHP applications and experiences from their use would still be applicable in a SBTVD/Ginga environment, even though the specific underlying technology would be different.

2.3 Local Technical Environment

As part of another IST project, named Opera[3], a PLC[4] network has been installed in parts of Barreirinhas. (That PLC network was connected via a WiMAX link to the server system at main government building, though this was transparent as far as the use in the SAMBA project was concerned.)

The PLC network was used as the back channel for the SAMBA set-top boxes, providing good connectivity between the participating households and the server. (An overview is given in figure 1.) However, there was no high-speed link to the outside Internet. There was a satellite link available at the government building (which is a standard feature for all mayors offices in Brazil), which could be used

[3] Open PLC European Research Alliance.
[4] Power Line Communication.

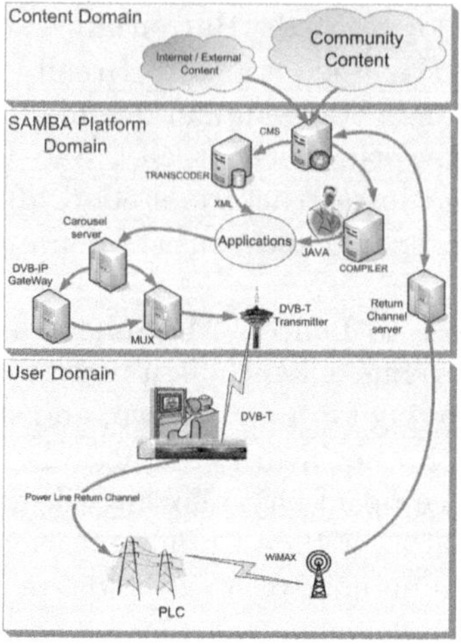

Fig. 1. Overview of SAMBA communication structure

by the SAMBA project, but the bandwidth available for the project was limited and it was insufficient to provide 'regular' Internet access for the households involved in the project.

3 Project Goals

Based on the technology available, the goal of the project was to develop, test and showcase 'Internet-like' applications that could be used on a commercially available MHP set-top box, keeping the cost for the box below 100 US$.

While it was agreed that it would be preferable to use low-cost computers and direct Internet access, given the local income structure, the price difference between a set-top box and a computer was significant. Additionally, with the move from analogue to digital television and an expected discontinuation of analogue services in 2016, it is expected that residents will be more likely to invest in set-top boxes first, especially since TV services are considered more relevant than Internet services.

Since outside access to the Internet was limited, it was decided to put more emphasis on local and user generated content than originally intended and provide only news as external information.

Based on field studies among the potential users where researchers found out the following order of needs and expectations of the community:

- *Interaction*
- *Information*
- *Education*
- *Entertainment*

For local users the capability of interacting within the community was of higher importance than using it as a means of information. The users' interest in creating local content and in visualizing and sharing it through TV screen is linked to the fact that television is typically the only vehicle of information for many of the townspeople. Providing the technical means for local interaction was seen as an enabler for information and education and entertainment as well.

4 Application Selection

Services from various areas were considered, including health and government information, community blackboard, price information for local shops, tourist guide, gaming, voting, e-mail, online chat and photo gallery.

Some of these services were equivalent from a technical point of view, since most services that only need to present information on the screen (whether this is shopping, health, sports club or local community information) can be handled by a single application, as long as the visual appearance can be adapted to the specific service.

Other services were difficult to implement, given the constraints of a set-top box. While e-mail was one of the more desirable features from a user point of view, the set-top box did not have any keyboard due to cost considerations, so the users would have to 'type' e-mails by using a virtual on-screen keyboard, which was cumbersome. (Due to user requests, an SMS (texting) service was implemented instead.)

It was decided to implement four applications (plus one additional cross-application function), in order to demonstrate a sufficiently wide range of services and scenarios.

- *Photo Gallery*
  This allowed users to upload images from a regular PC, which were then viewable on the set-top box. Intended users were local teachers and sports fans, who could take pictures at school and sports events and make them available for general viewing.
- *Info application*
  The info application was a generic application for the presentation of individual information pages and the navigation between them. This was used for a variety of services. The basic data per page was intentionally kept simple (a text block, an image, navigation hints for previous, next and upper level page). To provide variety , as well as providing users a sense of which 'region' of the navigation tree they were in, the layout of the pages was modifiable, so that the appearance of news would differ from the appearance of local event information.
- *Polls*
  This application allowed users to post multiple choice questions for a specific timeframe and collect and view responses.
- *SMS*
  This function allowed the sending of text messages to mobile phones. It was included upon specific request of the users.

– *Alert-Function*
  In addition to the four application, an alert function was added to the system, allowing the presentation of an alert message on the user's TV (specific users could be addressed, as well as all users). Due to the disruptive nature of the feature, it was only intended for emergencies.

All application interfaces were implemented to be switchable between Portuguese, Italian and English, so that they could be used in the Brazilian testbed, an Italian testbed and on international presentations.

5 Application Development

Due to the strong emphasis on services for the local community, users were involved early in the project. A group of HCI[5] experts from the University in Fortaleza, together with other Brazilian partners in the project, visited Barreirinhas to present the project to local users and gather user demographics and information about their needs and requirements.

To avoid working with abstract information during development, the demographics were condensed to six 'personas', representing typical users in various age groups. These personas were given detailed descriptions, including professions, preferences, technical experiences and goals, as well as (comic-style) representations. For internal project use, real users were then mapped to the closest persona.

During the project, a number of visits were made to Barreirinhas to present the applications in various prototype stages and elicit suggestions and feedback from the users.

Making the users feel part of the project was an important goal. Meetings were not only focused on demo applications but also on establishing a relationship between developers and users. This allowed developers gaining credibility and the involvement of the local organization, content creators and users. Consequently, the users were easily persuaded to create local content by applying collaborative strategies.

Prototypes shown to the users started with hand-drawn story boards showing the planned use of the application, followed by PowerPoint presentations of simplified application views (just grey boxes and texts), then PowerPoint presentation of the applications with proper design and layout, functional demonstrations of the applications in a set-top box emulator and finally a presentation of the near-finished application on an actual set-top box, before delivering the boxes to the users at home.

Beside the obvious advantage of involving users early, which is getting feedback on the applications, it also helped the project in a number of additional ways.

– Users were involved regularly during the course of the project, keeping them interested in the project.

[5] Human Computer Interaction.

Fig. 2. Hand drawn storyboard for photo application

Fig. 3. Left: Simplified application view **Right:** Final application

- Users could see the effect of their suggestions on the development of the applications.
- Involving users continuously helped to build a community, which furthered user created content after deployment of the application.
- Establishing a way of communicating user requests to the developers early in the project helped setting up a 'communication pipeline' across spatial, linguistic and cultural distances, which improved communication during the user trials.
- During the content creation process, rules were generally followed and there were no problems with copyright violations and inappropriate content, which is often a problem with (relatively) openly accessible Content Management Systems.

6 Content Creation

Content for the applications came from three sources, RSS feeds, local content providers and users.

6.1 RSS Feeds

For news and other general information, an RSS reader was installed that accessed the news feed of a Brazilian newspaper and automatically converted the information to a format suitable for the info application before storing it in the local CMS[6].

By using this method, we could ensure that the use of the satellite link was limited to incremental hourly updates and would be independent of the usage patterns of the info applications.

6.2 Local Content Providers

To add content to the info, photo and vote application, Java applets and applications were written. Since these could not be used on the set-top box, they could be accessed from a PC at the office of a local organisation[7] associated with the project.

Pages for the info application containing information from local businesses, groups and government institutions and the questions and choices for various polls were entered from this PC.

Three local organizations were involved in creating content to promote digital and social inclusion by providing educational, business and tourism information.

6.3 User Created Content

Local users could access the PC designated for content creation to add their own content. This was mainly intended to allow users to upload images taken with digital cameras to the photo application, which could not be performed from home due to the lack of USB or SD card ports on the set-top boxes. Users were also able to create pages for the info application and polls for the poll application.

Since the only available input device on the set-top box was the remote control, opportunities for content creation at the users homes was limited. However, it was possible to write SMS messages and send them to mobile phones and to rate photos in galleries and add one-line comments to them.

[6] Content Management System.

[7] SEBRAE, a Brazilian service for the support of small businesses.

6.4 User Training

To enable users in the community to create their own content, two tutorials were given. The first tutorial was given to the local content providers and consisted of a one day tutorial of the content creation tools available at the PC. This tutorial consisted of a short introduction to the tools, followed by a 'hands on' session to create actual content pages. At the end of the day, a questionnaire was used to gather user comments and suggestions.

Fig. 4. Tutorial for local content providers

Fig. 5. Creation of digital content from source material

For the end home users, a two hour tutorial of the set-top box and the use of the applications on the box were given. To learn about adding their own content, if desired, they were referred to local content providers that had finished the one day tutorial.

7 Lessons Learned

While some of the experiences from the SAMBA project are specific to the situation in Barreirinhas, there are a number of issues that can probably be applied to other communities.

The most important characteristic of Barreirinhas is that it is essentially an urban, not a rural environments. This made the use of DVB-T practical, since it has a comparatively small reception footprint, making it less suitable for rural communities. It also allowed to separate 'content creation' from the end users systems, which were set-top boxes with limited input facilities, by providing a central PC for creating content and uploading photographs, which might have been less acceptable for the user community, if the office with the PC had not been literally 'around the corner'.

7.1 Lack of Keyboard

In the planning stages of the project, the lack of a keyboard was seen as a potential problem and it was considered providing a keyboard with the set-top box, but that would have raised the cost of the box substantially., In the course of the project the non-availibility of a keyboard for the set-top boxes did not have a significant negative effect. Due to the small urban area covered, using the central PC to add photos or longer pages was not a problem and most comments to photographs were just one or two words anyway (the equivalent of 'nice picture' or 'great') or just a rating from one to five stars. Longer comments were rarely given and the short phrases seemed enough to instil a feeling of community.

7.2 MHP

As the system for the end user applications, MHP was a useful tool, primarily due to being the only standardised system that was low cost and allowed the use a mixture of content from the broadcast stream and from the back channel.

As a presentation tool, it had the disadvantage of requiring every application to be written specifically for MHP, limiting the number of applications that could be provided by the project.

A more Web-friendly technology, such as CE-HTML (a HTML variant aimed at consumer electronic devices like TVs) or some other variation of HTML plus some scripting language would have allowed a mix of existing applications and those written specifically for the project. For example, a user request was to provide an interface to Orkut (a service, popular in Brazil, which is similar to Facebook), which could not be provided in MHP, but could easily be provided in most HTML variants.

At the start of the project, however, there were no sufficiently affordable set-top boxes that allowed the display of HTML pages from the broadcast stream.

7.3 Limited Internet

The primary request of users was to have 'the Internet on their TV'. This was not possible due to two reasons.

1. The MHP set-top box had no full-scale browser, so only content converted specifically for the MHP applications could be presented, but no arbitrary pages from the Web.
2. Only a limited bandwidth was available through the satellite link, so that only content cached at the community server could be made available, but no direct access to the outside line.

While a full browser would have been desirable, no system costing less than 100$ was available during the course of the project. Using a more expensive system would have defeated the purpose of the project (making features available to low income communities). With specific media processors and falling prices, browsing-capable low-cost set-top boxes seem likely to appear within a year.

This still leaves the problem of providing sufficiently large bandwidth to the Internet, but even just a server for communication within the local community fulfilled a large number of requirements.

The use of the Internet falls clearly into two different categories. The first is the Web 1.0 usage, which is mainly characterized by information gathering and could not be provided within the project except for a rudimentary way. Web 2.0 usage, however, which is mainly characterized by community building, did work well, even in a simplified form, since the primary community, even in the Internet, tends to be the local community of relatives and friends, which could be reached with a local network.

References

1. SAMBA Project Homepage, `http://www.ist-samba.eu/`
2. Mayora, O., Costa, C.: The SAMBA Approach to Community-Based Interactive Digital Television. In: Proceedings of ChinaCom Conference, Shanghai, China (August 2007)
3. Mayora, et al.: User Centric Media in the Future Internet: Trends and Challenges. In: ACM DIMEA conference, Athens, Greece (September 2008)
4. Souza, G.L., Leite, L.E.C., Batista, C.E.C.F.: Ginga-J: Middleware for the Brazilian Digital TV System
5. Furtado, E., Kampf, T., Piccolo, L., Baranauskas, M.C.C.: Prospecting the Appropriation of the Digital TV in a Brazilian Project. In: Tscheligi, M., Obrist, M., Lugmayr, A. (eds.) EuroITV 2008. LNCS, vol. 5066, pp. 293–302. Springer, Heidelberg (2008)

E-Voting: A South African Perspective

E. Swanepoel, K. Thomson, and J.F. van Niekerk

School of ICT, Nelson Mandela Metropolitan University

Abstract. The South African democracy, despite being worthy of admiration, is in its infancy. As such its electoral processes still needs to be nurtured and protected. Since 1994 there has been four national elections. All of these have been declared "free and fair" by the Independent Electoral Commission. However, there has been some problems and growing pains. This paper firstly discusses the current electoral system in South Africa. It then examines E-voting systems and discusses the feasibility of such a voting system for use in the South African context.

1 Introduction

"The victory of democracy in South Africa is the common achievement of all humanity." [Mandela(2005)].

Democracy is one of South Africa's biggest achievements. Fifteen years ago, for the first time, all South Africans had the right to cast their vote. This included people of all cultures. Since 1994 South Africa has had four national elections considered to be "free and fair" by the Independent Electoral Commission (IEC) of South Africa.

However, elections are not by default "free and fair". It is the responsibility of the IEC to ensure the continued integrity of the South African electoral system. The "fairness" of an election is determined by a combination of factors, including people, processes and the system itself. Occasionally this system comes under attack from unscrupulous individuals. For example, in the 2009 election marked national and provincial ballot papers were found sealed in envelopes in KwaZulu-Natal before the elections actually took place [News24(2009)]. It would be naive to assume that similar attempts at influencing the vote would not occur in future elections. The process of voting in South Africa is questioned by some, how "free and fair" is the final result? [Ebersohn(2009)]. Not everyone in South Africa can experience democracy and receive the benefits from such a system. For example citizens visiting foreign countries, people with disabilities, and people with transport problems in rural areas do not necessarily have easy access to polling stations. There have also been reported cases of multiple votes being cast [Ebersohn(2009)]. This paper will examine the South African election system and discuss the viability of E-voting in South Africa as a way to improve the overall efficiency of the system, and to reduce the risk of future attacks on the integrity of the system.

A. Villafiorita, R. Saint-Paul, and A. Zorer (Eds.): AFRICOMM 2009, LNICST 38, pp. 70–77, 2010.

2 Background on the South African Electoral System

Microsoft Encarta Encyclopedia Online defines democracy as "the free and equal right of every person to participate in a system of government often practiced by electing representatives of the people by the majority of the people." [Encarta(2009)].

In December 1993, the South African government permitted equal rights to all South African citizens [Athiemoolam(2003)]. South Africa's first fully democratic election was held between 26 and 29 April 1994. The Independent Electoral Commission (IEC), which included international observers, declared that South Africa had a free and fair election [lvarez Rivera(2006)]. Looking at South African history, having such efficient transition to democracy can be seen as a miracle. This event captured the attention of people all around the world [Athiemoolam(2003)].

After the first democratic election the government prescribed a constitution which has been called the "birth certificate" of a new South Africa. Chapter One of the constitution guarantees democracy in South Africa; every South African citizen over the age of 18 has the right to vote in the South African elections [Republic of South Africa(1996)]. This corresponds to the vision statement of the Independent Electoral Commission stating that South Africa should have a "free and fair" election giving every voter the opportunity to vote for his/her chosen parties [IEC(2004)]. The IEC has been responsible for the implementation of the electoral system for the elections in South Africa since the first democratic election in 1994.

The South African parliamentary election takes place every five years with elections held under an electoral system of proportional representation. A proportional system uses a political party list at provincial and national levels. The political party will be allocated a number of seats in direct proportion to the number of votes received in the election. The voter can only vote for a party not an individual of choice. To ensure a "free and fair" election the electoral commission of South Africa oversees the election process [IEC(2004)].

The IEC is a permanent body established in terms of the Electoral Commission Act of 1996. It is independent from government, but reports to Parliament. The IEC promotes democracy in South Africa and must ensure a "free and fair" election at all levels of government - national, provincial and local. This is accomplished through:

- Dividing South Africa into voting districts, this ensures equal access to polling stations and avoids problems associated with overcrowding;
- Arranging the logistics of the election. This includes Information Technology systems, staffing, management of conflicts and the education of voters;
- Registering eligible voters onto a voters roll;
- Ensuring the efficiency of running the voting process; and
- Counting, verifying and announcing the final results of elections [IEC(2004)].

As can be seen from this list of tasks the IEC is responsible for overseeing the whole election process and contributing to a "free and fair" election.

3 Electoral System Characteristics

In South Africa, since 1999 eligible voters had to register to cast a vote in elections. The 1999 election saw 18 172 751 voters register in 14 650 voting districts. In 2004, 20 674 926 voters registered in 16 966 voting districts and in 2009, 23 181 997 voters registered in 19 705 voting districts. Prior to the current voting process, voters were allowed to cast their vote without having to be on a voter's roll. The current process in South Africa allows the voter to cast a vote on a ballot paper using a pencil selecting a political party [IEC(2004)].

The cost of the physical ballot paper is the first identified characteristic. In the 2004 election 56 million ballot papers were printed in colour with the 11 official languages on the ballot papers. As per the EISA research report no. 12, the total cost of the 2004 election was R790 million - that is R50.59 per national vote. The 1999 election cost R713.5 million or R44.65 per national vote; and 1994 cost R960 million or R49.15 per national vote [Piper(2005)].

A possible drawback to the South Africa system is that there are a large number of illiterate adults. Statistics show that 24 % of adults in South Africa over the age of 15 are illiterate. The number of languages in South Africa can contribute to further problems when voters go to the polling stations. Casting a vote using a ballot form might sound simple for educated people, but for illiterate people this can be a challenging task [SouthAfrica.info(2006)]).

In addition, the Electoral Institute of South Africa recognized in the 2004 elections that some of the ballot papers were not clear and contributed to some confusion amongst voters which could have played a part in the 1,58 % spoilt ballots. In the 2009 election there were 239,237 spoilt ballots nationally and 223,462 provincially [IEC(2004)].

Another concern is confidence in the ballot form. According to a survey done by Citizen Surveys in October and November 2008, South African citizens were concerned that the secrecy of their ballot form could be compromised. A sample was conducted on 2400 South Africans revealing that 58 % had confidence in the secrecy of their ballot form (Concern about Ballot Secrecy, online). In a report delivered by the Electoral Institute of South Africa, the 2009 election showed that a large number of the election officials did not have a clear understanding of the counting process which lead to delays. They observed that some of the polling stations used one ballot box for both ballots; the national assembly and provincial legislatures. Also the seals on some ballot boxes were not applied using the correct procedures [EIS(2009)].

A further contributing drawback is the fact that poverty is one of South Africa's biggest challenges, 50 % of the population live in underprivileged conditions [wor(2009)]. Transport from rural areas to polling stations can decrease voting registration and participation. People may not have the necessary funds to travel to an election polling station, which can be the reason for voter turnout decreasing in the South African elections. In 1994, 84 % of eligible voters cast their vote. In the 1999 election that figure declined to 63 % and in 2004, the election had a 61 % turnout [Kersting(June 2007)].

People with disabilities can face some disadvantages when it comes to casting votes, depending on their disability. In South Africa there are approximately 4 million people with disabilities according to the Council for Scientific and Industrial Research. As an example; when a blind person, or some one else with a disability, has to rely on assistance when casting his/her vote by making use of the presiding officer at the voting station; the integrity of the vote might be influenced [IEC(2009a)].

A large percentage of South African citizens live abroad and were eligible to take part in the 2009 election. The Constitutional Court delivered this decision on 12 March 2009 allowing South Africans living abroad to vote in the 2009 elections [IEC(2009b)]. This is good for democracy in South Africa, but can lead to challenges such as voters having problems accessing an embassy to register and cast their vote.

South Africans should not only be able to vote, but should also have a system that can be trusted. The protection of information in an election is very important; therefore this information needs to be protected from threats [Von Solms and Von Solms(2008)]. The risks that threaten the confidentiality, integrity and availability of information must be mitigated or fully eliminated. This will contribute to having a "free and fair" election where voters will have confidence in their country's electoral system.

A possible solution to eliminate some of these challenges facing the electoral system in South Africa is making use of technology; the implementation of an electronic voting system.

4 Background on Electronic Voting Systems

Electronic voting is the use of electronic means to cast a vote and is also know as E-voting. Since 1960 electronic systems have been used in certain states in America and more recently remote electronic voting has been used in countries like Estonia, Switzerland and others. E-voting is meant to complement traditional voting methods. There are different types of E-voting methods, including punch cards, optical scan voting systems, direct recording electronic voting systems (DRE systems), Web-based voting systems, ballots and voting via telephone [Bellis(Undated)][Gritzalis(2002)].

4.1 Punch Card Voting Systems

Punch cards is a voting system that has been around for decades where the voter still has to go to a polling station to cast his/her vote. This method of voting makes use of a small clipboard-sized device with a card where the voter's choice is recorded on. The card slides into the device and uses a metal or stylus device to make a hole next to the political party or candidate of his/her choice. The ballot will then be tabulated with a card counter at the polling station or at a central location using card readers. There are two well known versions of this voting system i.e. votomatic vote recorder and the datavote vote recorder [Bellis(Undated)][Gritzalis(2002)].

4.2 Direct Record Voting Systems

Direct record electronic voting systems are also known as a DRE voting system. DRE systems are the electronic version of the older mechanical lever system. They are similar because both systems don't use ballot papers to record a vote on. The DRE voting machines have touch screens or make use of keyboards to cast a vote electronically. The DRE machine has a monitor that guides the voter through all the steps involved in an election. All the votes that have been made by voters are stored on the voting machines. Storage methods used are for example memory cartridges, diskettes or smart cards. DRE systems are one of the most recent additions in the development of E-voting systems i.e. using technology to cast a vote in an election [Bellis(Undated)][Gritzalis(2002)]. DRE voting systems could have many advantages in a South African context. For example; the use of such systems could help to address the problems associated with having eleven official languages, or, by paying attention to usability concerns, a DRE could also be customized to alleviate problems experienced by disabled voters. These, and many other possible advantages, could make DRE voting systems a viable option in future.

4.3 Optical Scan Voting Systems

An optical scan voting system makes use of "dark magic logic"; this is used to read a voter's ballot form by selecting the darkest mark on the form as the choice of vote. The voter will cast a vote on a ballot form, where the political party or candidate is pre-printed with an empty rectangle, circle, oval or arrow next to it. Selecting a political party or candidate of choice is done by filling in the empty rectangle, circle, oval or arrow. The voter will then feed this ballot form into a computer tabulating system to be counted. The ballot form can also be placed in a ballot box where it will be counted by electoral staff. Making use of the optical-scan machines at the polling station will give you confidence that your vote was counted immediately. Optical scan technology has been used for decades not only for voting, but also implemented in worldwide lottery systems [Bellis(Undated)][Gritzalis(2002)].

4.4 Internet Voting System

Internet-, or Web-based voting systems, is another electronic method of voting referred to as remote electronic voting. Remote electronic voting requires that the voter has access to an Internet connection. Some countries for example Austria, Canada, Switzerland and others are involved in running pilot projects for implementing a remote electronic system in their election. Estonia became the first country to use remote electronic voting in their elections. In Estonia a voter needs to have an electronic identification card. The voting process consists of the following; first the voter inserts the identification card into a card reader, a webpage opens where the voter will cast his/her vote. The voter will need to enter a PIN for verification and a server checks the credentials of the voter. The server will also verify that the voter is eligible to cast his/her vote. After verification a list of the candidates appears and the voter can make his/her choice, this will be encrypted. A second PIN is required to confirm the selection using a digital signature. Security in a remote electronic system is very important for an election. Making use of the Internet gives a voter the opportunity to cast their vote from anywhere in the world giving everyone the opportunity to participate [Estonia Today(2009)].

5 Electronic Voting Characteristics

E-voting enables new methods of polling, which facilitates the comfort of voters, increases the opportunity to participate and the mobility of voters. This would be particularly beneficial for those citizens who live abroad, have transport problems or are disabled and consequently limited in terms of mobility. E-voting can be beneficial for voter turnout; potentially everyone would be able to take part in the election and easier election participation would be possible. Groups of people that will benefit would be, for example, young people that are increasingly using the Internet and older people that have mobility problems. Citizens living overseas will also have the ability to vote as access to the Internet is available worldwide [Brändli and Braun(2006)].

The current South African electoral system has some drawbacks and introducing E-voting could possibly help improve the system. E-voting can help with the reduction of ballot paper and employment cost in an election and contribute to reducing environmental effects by reducing paper consumption. The counting process and result tabulation when using E-voting will much faster. Initially, the E-voting system may be more costly to implement. However, the high cost of printing ballot papers would be eliminated. Therefore in the long term, once fully implemented, E-voting could prove to be more financially viable. In addition to these cost savings, issues such as ballot box shortages that occurred in the 2009 election will be something of the past.

With approximately 1.5 million South Africans living abroad the use of Internet voting will give the opportunity to expats to cast their vote from anywhere in the world. This is not only beneficial to expats but disabled people would benefit from this too. Disabled individuals could make use of headphones, Braille keypads and so forth to cast their votes and they can vote within the comfort of their own home. This will allow them to vote independently, no human aide needed and contribute to the integrity of the vote.

Another benefit would be that the voter can change his/her vote if needed before polling station closure. Addressing the useability of such an E-voting system would be very important. South Africa has a large number of people that are illiterate; this can be one of the biggest challenges when it comes to E-voting in South African. An E-voting system can be developed with a graphical user interface making it user friendly. This will make it possible for illiterate people to understand and be able to cast a vote. Another added feature when using E-voting is that it can accommodate multiple languages thus giving every voter access in their own language. With South Africa having 11 official languages this contributes to improving the useability of such a system.

However, with these added benefits, come increased security requirements. It is vital that the confidentiality, integrity and availability of election information must be protected to ensure the public's confidence. This is also one of the challenges facing the use of such an E-voting system. The worse-case scenario can have a devastating effect on an election. Protecting information is a challenge because of all the risks that technology faces. Examples are viruses, hackers, physical tampering, spoofing and so forth [Rubin(2002)]. Protecting a user's anonymity is very important for such an electronic system. The voter needs to know that their vote is confidential. By achieving this, confidence in such an electoral system will increase. Everyone involved in an election, including the voter, politicians and authorities need to trust the system [Brändli and Braun(2006)].

6 Conclusion

This paper has shown that there are still problems in the electoral system currently being used in South Africa. Many of these problems could conceivably be alleviated through the implementation of a comprehensive E-voting system. However, despite the possible benefits of such a system, one could also argue that South Africa is not yet ready for such a system. Apart from infrastructure questions, which should be investigated in future studies, one should also ask whether or not the South African public is ready for such a change. South Africans have only recently started to trust and make use of online services, such as, online banking, online gambling, buying airline tickets, paying accounts, filing tax returns, etc. Without public confidence, E-voting would not work. It would thus be imperative to comprehensively address the security concerns, which include issues of human confidence, before such a system is considered for South Africa. It could be argued that initial attempts should focus on using a combination of traditional and E-voting systems.

It should, however, be clear that a lot more research is needed before the question: "Is South Africa ready for E-voting?", can be answered. Future research will focus on addressing this question.

References

[EIS(2009)] Interim statement: Eisa observer mission to the 2009 south african national & provincial elections. Internet (2009)

[IEC(2009a)] Voting questions and answers. Internet (2009a)

[IEC(2004)] Report on the national and provincial elections. Technical report, Independent Electoral Commission (2004)

[wor(2009)] World bank: South africa - country brief. Internet (2009)

[Athiemoolam(2003)] Athiemoolam, L.: South africa's peaceful transition to democracy: Nine years of peace in a trouble world. In: Peace as a Global Language Conference II, Seisen University, Tokyo, September 27-28 (2003), `http://www.zsn.uni-oldenburg.de/download/Logan_Japan_Conference.pdf` (retrieved March 29, 2009)

[Bellis(Undated)] Bellis, M.: The history of voting machines. [WWW document], `http://inventors.about.com/library/weekly/aa111300b.htm` (retrieved March 3, 2009) (Undated)

[Brändli and Braun(2006)] Brändli, D., Braun, N.: Swiss e-voting pilot projects: Evaluation, situation analysis and how to proceed (2006), `http://www.e-voting.cc/static/evoting/files/braun_braendli_swiss_e-voting_27%-36.pdf` (retrieved March 3, 2009)

[Ebersohn(2009)] Ebersohn, K.: Bloemfonteinse vrou kry dit reg om twee keer te stem. Internet (2009)

[Encarta(2009)] Encarta. Democracy. Internet (2009)

[Estonia Today(2009)] Estonia Today. Estonia e-voting system. Internet (2009)

[Gritzalis(2002)] Gritzalis, D.: Secure Electronic Voting. Springer (2002)

[IEC(2009b)] IEC. Constitutional court ruling on overseas voting. [WWW document] (2009b), `http://www.elections.org.za/news.asp?press=0Opt=Data=Recnum=21` (retrieved March 13, 2009)

[Kersting(June 2007)] Kersting, N.: Electoral reform in southern africa: voter turnout, electoral rules and infrastructure. Journal of African Elections 6(1), 134–151 (2007)

[lvarez Rivera(2006)] Álvarez Rivera, M.: The republic of south africa electoral system. [WWW document] (2006), `http://www.electionresources.org/za/system/` (retrieved March 29, 2009)

[Mandela(2005)] Mandela, N.: Long Walk to Freedom. Abascus (2005)

[News24(2009)] News24. Marked ballot papers found. Internet (2009)

[Piper(2005)] Piper, L.: South Africa's 2004 Election: The Quest for Democratic Consolidation. EISA, South Africa (2005)

[Republic of South Africa(1996)] Republic of South Africa. Constitutional court of south africa. [WWW document] (1996), `http://www.constitutionalcourt.org.za/site/theconstitution/whatisaconstitution.htm`(retrieved March 29, 2009)

[Rubin(2002)] Rubin, A.: Security considerations for remote electronic voting. Communications of the ACM 45(12), 39–44 (2002)

[SouthAfrica.info(2006)] SouthAfrica. info. Education in south africa. Internet (2006)

[Von Solms and Von Solms(2008)] Von Solms, R., Von Solms, B.: Information Security Governance. Springer, Heidelberg (2008)

BoulSat Project: Low-Cost Wireless Metropolitan Network Implementation in Burkina Faso

Samuele S. Catusian[1], Federico Longobardi[2], Francesco Panicucci[1], Raphael P. Bartalesi[1], Libertario Demi[1], Antonio D. Cuomo[1], and Silvano Orlandi[3]

[1] Ingegneria Senza Frontiere - Pisa
http://isf-pisa.org/
[2] Ingegneria Senza Frontiere - Torino
http://isf.polito.it/
[3] Centro Sviluppo Umano ONLUS
http://csuonlus.org/

Abstract. The BoulSat Project involves the realization of a bidirectional VSAT (satellite connection system) and the study of "poor" a Wireless Metropolitan Area Network (WMAN) to extend the Internet connectivity to the public institutions in the town area. Low-cost or waste materials have been used to build components where possible, thus to make possible for the local technicians with no specific and theoretical skills to build their network components by hand. This pilot scheme has been applied in Boulsa, in the Sahel region at the north of Burkina Faso. Besides the Boulsa case study, the whole work analyses a typical situation, due to the wide range of problems which have been handled, of remote communities in the South of the World. The aim is to characterize a standard of intervention, suitable for Developing Countries, to set up low-cost wireless telecommunication infrastructures.

Keywords: poor-wlan, digital divide, telecommunications infrastructures, wireless networks, wi-fi/hyperlan, technology transfer.

1 Introduction

According to the UN reports[1], Burkina Faso (ex Alto Volta, a former French colony) is one of the poorest countries in the world. Boulsa is the main city of the Namentenga province, situated in the north-east region at about 190 km from the capital city Ouagadougou. According to the local statistics, the Namentenga is the poorest district among the country, counting more than 300'000 inhabitants. The Nasongdo[2] Association has been one of the Project main partners. Born in Boulsa in the sixties it is now a recognized NGO with more than a thousand associates organized in 50 more groups, engaged in a plethora of

[1] For more informations refer to: World Health Organization WHOSIS, UNICEF, World Development Indicators database (World Bank sources of data).
[2] *Help ourself* in the local Moore language.

A. Villafiorita, R. Saint-Paul, and A. Zorer (Eds.): AFRICOMM 2009, LNICST 38, pp. 78–85, 2010.

different development activities in various fields: alphabetization, water access, agriculture, basic professional courses and digital divide among the others.

The BoulSat Project[2] was originated from a request conveyed by Centro Sviluppo Umano ONLUS [3], an Italian no-profit association which has been active in the Namentenga district since 1999. The first contact between ISF/EWB Italian network[1] and Nasongdo was so established in 2005.

1.1 Need of Telecommunications in the Context Scenario

The first question coming to mind could be: is there a real need of an Internet connection in such context? The answer may seem trivial, but it is not. At least, not always. Presently, we deem none has valid and absolute answer to the question: access to information and communication is intended as a necessary condition to reach medium and/or long term development goals, but indeed it is not sufficient. Lots of other pre-conditions are necessary, thus we deem each case has to be really well evaluated in its particularity.

As of august 2005, the main city of Boulsa was provided with decent electrical energy, mobile phone coverage was work-in-progress and landlines were slightly stable just for voice calls. In fact the ONATEL[3] central telephone exchange is not actually connected to the national telecommunication network neither via a fibre optic nor with the old copper twisted pair cable. Instead there is an old and overloaded medium frequency radio bridge with the capital city. Neither wired nor wireless improvement were/are planned on the infrastructure, and the telephone exchange is full, making really difficult to have a new line activated. The existing ones are suffering due to the unreliability of the radio connection between the telephone exchange and the rest of the national network, so Internet access was only possible via slow PSTN (analog) modems connected to the telephone line (if any), prone to signal degradation and to very frequent call droppings, especially in the rainy season.

2 Materials and Methods

In this scenario, the aim of the BoulSat project was to bring the Internet connection to Nasongdo offices and laboratories and to share it to the hospital, the Health Administration, the Town Hall. The technical subjects of study were two different and well identified problems. To guarantee the access to a wide Internet band, and to design a distribution network to cover the town area with Internet services.

Instead to implement a standard wireless network with common commercial components, ISF worked on an easy replicable and very low cost solution using the materials available on-site[4]. We used recycled metal cans to develop and to optimize a home made sector antenna (Cantenna); dismantled water pipes were adopted to design and realize the antenna masts up to a height of

[3] Office Nationale de TELecomunication, the Burkinabè local telco (telecommunication company).

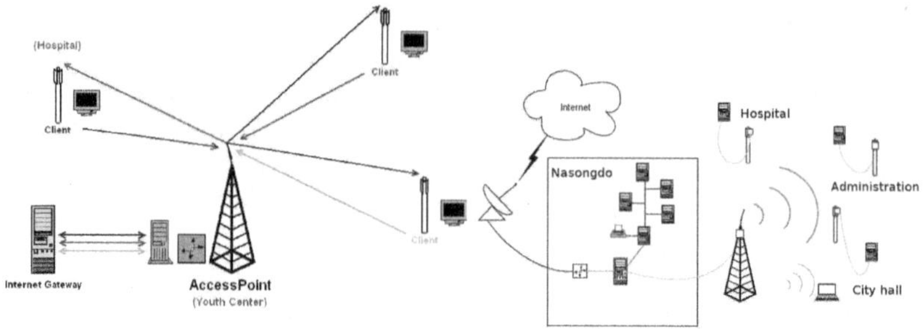

(a) (b)

Fig. 1. (a)A point-to-multipoint star topology to realize the distribution WMAN network; all the data-traffic pass through the central node which is located close to the satellite gateway; (b) The definitive network: WMAN and WLAN realize the metropolitan distribution network until the final wireless or wired user.

20 meters; self assembled low power, multi-standard transmitters complete the wireless infrastructure. For these reasons we defined our wireless network as *poor*.

The current configuration of the whole communication system is showed in figures 1(a) and 1(b). The satellite system is placed at the Nasongdo premises and it allows the local NGO offices and the computer laboratory to access the Internet. Then, by means of the point-to-multipoint WAN the three main nodes are linked: the Town Hall, the Hospital, and the Health Administration. An indoor/outdoor hotspot area in two of the connected nodes gives Internet and Intranet wireless access to local users without the need of a cabled network.

2.1 The Poor WLAN

As stated above, the distribution network must be very low cost, scalable, locally repeatable and easy to manage. The *Poor WLAN* (this name refers to the whole wireless network designed by the ISF team, WLAN and WMAN) is a proper solution to fulfil these requirements. Renouncing to the latest technologies for more stable and solid ones, by using open hardware/software and self-made components, the *Poor WLAN* allows to achieve the desired performances with rock-solid and very low-cost systems and offers a solution which is easy to manage and sustain for the local community.

The Poor WLAN solution consist of the following components:

1. self assembled wireless transmitters;
2. home-made sector antennas (Cantenna);
3. water-pipe antenna masts.

Each of this peculiarities is illustrated in detail it this paper.

2.2 The Wireless Transmitters

The so called transmitters represent the radio, routing and processing units of the wireless network. They have been implemented mounting proper wireless cards (mini-PCI devices) on rock-solid SBCs (single-board computers) which are highly integrated, fan-less and low power devices designed to run in harsh environments. A single board can supply one or more wireless cards realizing, on a single hardware, more transmitters working at different radio standards. The hardware is compliant with both open source and proprietary specific operating systems. The typical transmitter has small size (150 x 200 x 55 mm), low weight (less than 1 kg) and low power consumption (less than 23 W); it can be easily set up in different hostile environments and supplied by a small renewable energy system. The reliability is guaranteed by the few number of fan-less components (a single board computer and a radio card) closed in a proper outdoor-case shielded from any possible interference. In a typical set-up the transmitter is fixed on the mast near the antenna so to reduce the coaxial cable attenuation.

The power supply system can be positioned in a more convenient and safe location, typically inside the building at the base of the mast; the transmitter can be supplied with Power over Ethernet (PoE) technology. A final unit placed into a proper waterproof case and ready to be connected to one or more antennas, is shown in Fig. 2(a).

2.3 Home-Made Cantenna

One of the most innovative solution adopted by the Poor WLAN is the use of hand-made sector antenna. In our case study, but in many cases as well, the wireless distribution network includes cellular coverage over local areas (WLAN) and short/medium range point-to point or point-to-multipoint links between strategic locations (WMAN). A sector antenna is a compromise which fits very well in small scale distribution network, as for the town area of Boulsa, and can be used as the standard antenna.

The ISF team have worked to improve and standardize the known concept of Cantenna: an aperture antenna hand made by adapting a commercial metal can to a wave-guide. Two standard cans (Ballantines and Seed-Oil) have been chosen for their universal availability all over the world. The main goal has been to improve antenna gain and efficiency of radiation in a standard very low cost realization for Wi-Fi applications (within 2.4 GHz ISM frequency band) which can be easily reproduced everywhere and by everyone with a cost of about 2 Euro.

The final result is a sector antenna with an high efficiency of radiation, a gain of about 8 dBi and an Half Power Beam Width (HPBW) of about 60 degrees in both vertical and horizontal plane. Table 1 shows the measured matching performances of both Cantennas (Ballantines and Seed-Oil). The return loss values have been measured with a spectrum analyser within the Wi-Fi frequency band. The Voltage Standing Wave Ratio (VSWR) values have been calculated analytically, as it is shown in tables 1 and 2. The handmade Cantennas have an optimum efficiency of radiation which, for the Ballantines Can, is better than

(a) (b)

Fig. 2. (a) A self-assembled Hiperlan/Wi-Fi transmitter for local or metropolitan distribution networks. This prototype is implemented with a Mikrotik RouterBoard with a multi-standard wireless card on-board; (b) The Ballantine Cantenna measured in the anechoic chamber of the Politecnico of Torino.

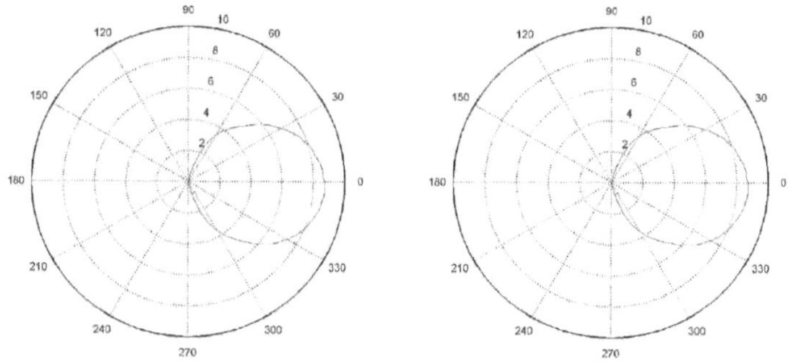

(a) (b)

Fig. 3. Measured gain in dB on (a) the vertical plane (E-plane) and (b) on the horizontal plane (H-plane)

99% at the centre frequency. In that condition more than 99% of the transmitted power from the wireless card is irradiated, almost without reflection back to the transmitter. This means high quality transmissions and low risk to damage the transmitter because of reflected power.

The best prototype, the Ballantines Cantenna, has been measured in the anechoic chamber of the Politecnico of Torino (Fig. 2(b)). Table 3 summarizes the relevant results which show the typical performance of a sector antenna. The measured gain pattern of both vertical and horizontal plane are illustrated respectively by figures 3(a) and 3(b).

Table 1. Measured Return Loss and calculated VSWR within the Wi-Fi frequency band for both prototypes of Cantenna

	@2.41GHz	*@2.44GHz*	*@2.48GHz*
(Ballantines Can) ***Return Loss*** ***VSWR***	 -22 dB 1.17	 -43 dB 1.02	 -22 dB 1.17
(Seed-oil Can) ***Return Loss*** ***VSWR***	 -15 dB 1.43	 -15 dB 1.38	 -13 dB 1.58

Table 2. Efficiency of radiation corresponding to different VSWR values; the percentage is relation to the transmitted power

VSWR	***Efficiency of radiation***
1.6	94.7%
1.4	97.2%
1.3	98.3%
1.2	99.2%

Table 3. Measured gain and Half Power Beam Width (HPBW) at the central frequency of the WiFi band; these values are relative of the Ballantines Cantennas

Ballantines Cantenna	***Gain***	***HPBW***
E-Plane	8.2 dB	68 degrees
H-Plane	8.7 dB	56 degrees

2.4 Low-Cost Antenna Mast

A demanding job has been to design and realize, together with the partner Nasongdo, simple and low-cost antenna masts in a brief time and with locally available materials. The required height was about 20 metres. A professional telecommunication mast of this size (a self supported or a monopole tower) was completely out of budget and also its shipment and assemblage would have required ulterior time and costs. The definitive idea was to assemble a very simple structure realized by properly welding together water pipes of six meters each, with steel connecting rods to guarantee the mast stability. This solution has the characteristic to be exclusively feasible with local materials, by the local community and consequently is very low-cost. Anyway there are also heavy drawbacks: this tower is not a modular structure and then it has to be raised up in one step; the construction material is not suitable for this purpose, it is heavy and this leads the mast to easily bend. The mast design does not provide any

(a) (b)

Fig. 4. (a) The cantenna with a PVC radome ready to be installed; all the material is low-cost, recycled and locally available; (b) The set up of an antenna mast made by water pipes (third expedition, Jan. 2007)

possibilities to set a grounding solution. Moreover this structure is not climbable and therefore all the wireless network equipment have to be fixed when the mast is down. The mast rising is a difficult and delicate phase; the risk of failure is not negligible. The mast dismounting for any maintenances is allowed only in emergency, i.e. when the system does not work at all. In Boulsa there was not any crane or other mechanical facility to rise up the mast, thus this operation has to be completely carried out by hand. At least thirty people were necessary for rising a mast (Fig. 4(b)).

According to the aforementioned drawbacks, a planned step in the system follow-up will be to substitute the pipe masts with appropriate antenna masts made by reticular modules allowing a relative easiness of the transmitter maintenance without loosing the robust concept of using locally available structural components.

2.5 Network Implementation

The first operating phase started in August 2006 when ISF implemented the VSAT system.

The second phase of the project consisted of the installation of the wireless infrastructure (Fig. 4(a)). This phase has been divided in some intermediate steps. First, ISF performed a technical site survey (August 2006) to know in detail the orographic and morphological characteristics of the area and to understand indications and expectations of the local community. Then, the entire technical solution was developed and tested in Italy by means of some trials and experimental wireless links. In January 2007 a second operating phase began. The main difficulties implementing the Poor WLAN concerned the set up and the management of the antenna masts, but after three weeks of work with local technicians all the nodes were connected with good performance: at least 5 Mbps of data-traffic over each wireless link. One year later the fourth expedition has been in charge of the monitoring of the system and further formation of the local technicians.

3 Results, Discussion and Future Developments

After two years from the first installation, the system is still running and usable. The satellite connection located at Nasongdo is working and the three node linked through the Poor WLAN are running. During this period some maintenance operations has been performed as periodic new pointing of the satellite antenna and the replacement of some electronic components which were damaged. On the whole the materials and the structures we used resisted to rains, wind and dust. However, the most important result we got is the involvement of the local community in using the new technology and the awareness they developed about it. For example, the employees of the health administration use the Internet connection to find up-to-date sanitary informations and communicate via e-mail. In general, the community exploits the new technology for communications (mail and VoIP), for education (computer science courses) and to support their work finding informations. This is important because the target of the project in the long term is to aid the development of the entire community.

Future developments concern the implementation of point-to-point wireless links over huge distances (more than 100 km). This is a key point of the whole project as this step would allow to transfer a wide band connection, for example a DSL, from a source location (for example the city of Koupela, about a hundred km in the south) to the remote area of Namentenga bypassing the VSAT links. For such cases we sized a photovoltaic system to be completely autonomous and relatively easy to build, transport and install, as described in [5]. This full wireless solution, independent from any satellite link, introduce relevant benefits if compared to the actual solution: wider bandwidth, much lower round trip times (which means possibility of efficient real-time services), higher reliability and scalability, full control and management of the whole telecommunication infrastructure, important economical save especially over long-term periods.

References

1. `http://isf-italia.org/`
2. BoulSat Project webpage
3. Centro Sviluppo Umano ONLUS, CSU, Viareggio, `http://csuonlus.org/`
4. Longobardi, F.: Boulsat Project - Radio network implementation by lowcost technology, Master Thesis
5. Bartalesi, R., Catusian, S., Cuomo, A., Longobardi, F., Panicucci, F.: SaharaWi-Fi Project - Low-cost full wireless connections over long distances in desert environment. In: 9th IEEE AFRICON (in press, 2009)

Telemedicine as a Tool for Europe-Africa Cooperation: A Practical Experience

Manuel Dinis[1], Fernando Santiago[2], Luís Silva[2], Ricardo Ferreira[2], José Machado[2], and Eduardo Castela[3]

[1] INOVETEL SA, Rua Amílcar Cabral nº 54 C, 1º Andar, Luanda, Angola
[2] PT Inovação SA, Rua Eng. José F. P. Basto, Aveiro, 3810-106, Portugal
[3] H. Pediátrico de Coimbra, Quinta dos Vales, S. Martinho do Bispo, Coimbra, Portugal
{manuel-dinis,santiago,luismiguel-h-silva,ricardo-j-ferreira, jose-e-machado}@ptinovacao.pt, ecastela@chc.min-saude.pt

Abstract. This paper presents the experience of an Europe-Africa telemedicine network, focused on the pediatric area, and involving hospitals located in Luanda (Angola), Benguela (Angola), Praia (Cape Verde) and Coimbra (Portugal). In the scope of this network, the cooperation between these hospitals goes beyond the teleconsultation sessions. Tele-training, clinical experience exchange, patient transfer agreements and health staff training to local development of new medical capabilities are some of the involved activities. It is therefore agreed that this kind of technical and knowledge network could also be expanded to other African countries with clear benefits to the local citizens, overcoming the digital-divide and improving the cooperation between developed and developing countries.

Keywords: telemedicine, telehealth, Africa, e-health, pediatric, cardiology, tele-echocardiography and telecommunications.

1 Introduction

Telemedicine is usually defined as the rapid access to remote medical expertise by means of telecommunications and information technologies regardless of where the patient, the physician and the relevant patient information are located [1]. Telemedicine has a surprisingly long history that began with the advent of the telephone. In 1906, Einthoven first investigated the chance to make use of electrocardiogram transmissions over telephone lines. In the 1920s, vessel radios were used to link physicians with sailors to assist during medical emergencies at sea. In 1955 the Nebraska Psychiatric Institute was among one of the first facilities to use closed-circuit television for healthcare purposes. In the 1970s, paramedics in remote Alaskan and Canadian villages were able to perform lifesaving techniques while linked with hospitals in distant towns using satellite communications. Today telemedicine is beginning to exponentially mature with the progressive advances in technology [1].

At the present time, by using modern telemedicine systems, various health related activities can be performed remotely, namely (1) teleconsultation, (2) telediagnostic

A. Villafiorita, R. Saint-Paul, and A. Zorer (Eds.): AFRICOMM 2009, LNICST 38, pp. 86–94, 2010.

and (3) telemonitoring. The first category encompasses a real time interaction between two physicians, or at least one physician and the patient, typically using advanced videoconference services. The second category, which can be performed in real time or in store&forward mode, involves the transmission of medical exams (video, image, sound, etc) to be observed by a remote specialist. The interest in real time transmission of medical data resides on the allowance of interactivity between physician(s) and patient and also by the fact that a faster and more accurate diagnostic of the pathology can be achieved. The last category corresponds to the remote continuous real time monitoring of patient's biological parameters.

The following advantages are commonly accepted for what concerns the benefits of telemedicine:

- Cost reduction and the process efficiency increase;
- Medical knowledge sharing and continuous training;
- Decrease on the number of patient transfers within hospitals;
- Decrease on the number of unnecessary hospitalizations;
- Availability of specialized services away from big urban centers;
- Better patient satisfaction due to faster and more accurate diagnostic.

The utilization of telemedicine systems seems especially suitable in the following cases:

- Initial and urgent assessment of patients in order to decide where they have to be transferred to specialized healthcare units;
- Rapid access to a specialized second opinion;
- Remote monitoring of post-hospitalization and post-surgical cases;
- Regular medical teleconsultations;
- Transmission of medical images for remote diagnostic;
- Continuous remote monitoring of risky patient status;
- Remote monitoring of patients with chronic diseases.

Worldwide there are many initiatives happening in the telemedicine or telehealth area. In Africa several initiatives have been reported, for instance in [2][3] and [4] several scenarios in sub-Saharan African countries are presented, namely within the RAFT project that has developed a telemedicine network, connecting healthcare centers at the French speaking countries, and supporting several activities like videoconferences, teleconsultations, collaborative knowledge bases development and distance continuous education. The communication infrastructure used by this network is based on Internet connections, and in some cases, satellite links (in rural areas).

In Portugal, a particularly interesting project was launched more than a decade ago by the R&D department of Portugal Telecom and the Pediatric Hospital of Coimbra. In 1998, this latter Hospital started a regular cardio-pediatrics teleconsultation service within Portugal, that turned a break evolution to around 2000 teleconsultations made in 2008 (just ten years after the service has been launched). Based on this experience, in 2007 this Hospital has extended its telemedicine reference service to some African countries, in order to exchange knowledge among Portuguese and African healthcare professionals and specially to aid young children with heart pathologies.

In this paper, the experience of this Europe-Africa pediatric-focused telemedicine network is described. The following sections present the chronology, technology, methodology and results of this telemedicine experience between Portugal, Cape Verde and Angola healthcare units.

2 Chronology

Launched in November of 2007, with the contribution of several public and private companies, PEDITEL pilot project aimed to aid the children with heart pathologies in Angola, as well as to adapt and promote the current technology capabilities to the Angola's territory. This project was also launched in cooperation with several Portuguese and Angolan institutions, namely: Pediatric Hospital of Luanda, Hospital of Benguela, Pediatric Hospital of Coimbra, Angola Telecom, Multitel, Unitel, HemoPortugal/HemoAngola and PT Inovação. The role of each of the partners on the project was dependent on its area of expertise, being the hospitals and its patients the final service end users. The telecommunication operators (Angola Telecom, Multitel and Unitel) provided the telecommunication infrastructures while PT Inovação provided the telemedicine system solution and HemoAngola provided some medical equipment. Within the time context of this pilot project, all the telemedicine solution equipment and communications was delivered at zero cost for the end users.

The main goals of this pilot project are to:

- Implement the basis for an integrated telemedicine solution in Angola (connecting Luanda and Benguela in its initial phase) for pediatric usage;
- Focus the telemedicine activities, at the beginning on the cardiology area and expand later to other medical areas;
- Identify and evaluate the use of the most cost effective telecommunications circuit solutions for the interconnection of the healthcare institutions;
- Test and evaluate the network behavior and reliability concerning the proposed services;
- Use the project resources also for training activities and evaluate its impact on the medical staff and the corresponding trainees;
- Evaluate a user friendly interface concerning the respective autonomy of the physicians when using the telemedicine equipment;
- Evaluate the impact and improvement on the corresponding medical services;
- Evaluate the business model that will enable a countrywide (in Angola) coverage of the service.

The implemented technical infrastructure is shown in Figure 1. It was installed a telemedicine workstation (Medigraf workstation) in each of the three hospitals, supporting videoconference, real-time teleconsultations, and real-time training activities. In terms of communications, the Pediatric Hospital of Luanda, Hospital of Benguela and Pediatric Hospital of Coimbra, were interconnected with 512 kbit/s dedicated point-to-point telecommunications circuits.

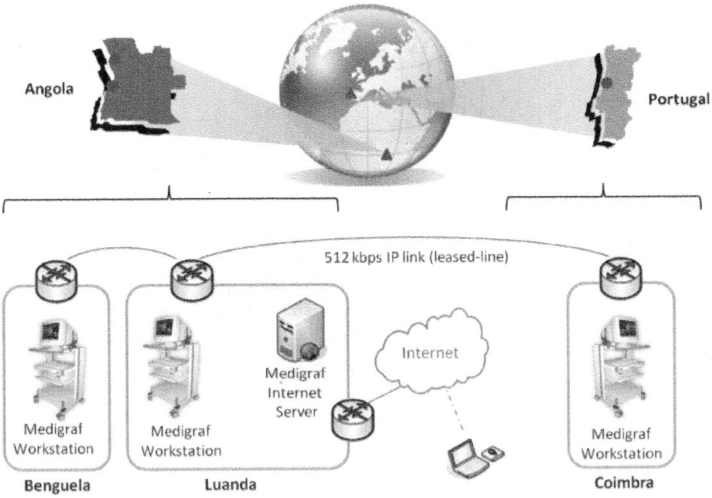

Fig. 1. PEDITEL telemedicine pilot project technical infrastructure

It was also installed the infrastructure (Medigraf Internet Server and network equipment) to allow the remote access of physicians, using a broadband Internet connection, to get and execute store-and-forward teleconsultations.

After an initial training period, making use of the telemedicine technology, the physicians started regular weekly real-time teleconsultations. The infrastructure was also successfully used for teletraining sessions and knowledge share meetings between Portuguese and Angolan healthcare professionals.

In May of 2009, given the experience obtained with this project in Angola, the Pediatric Hospital of Coimbra extended the telemedicine service to Hospital Dr. Agostinho Neto in Cape Verde. This service put in place for Cape Verde closed the gap between this islands needs and the medical offer available in Portugal. The scope of the Cape Verde project included medical staff training, patient evaluation and diagnostic previously to patient transfer to on-shore mainland Hospitals.

The telemedicine system that was installed at the Hospital Dr. Agostinho Neto, is similar to the one that was previously running in Angola healthcare units in the context of the PEDITEL project, however the communications infrastructure is based on ISDN lines in the Cape Verde project. The necessary bandwidth for real-time teleconsultations, is basically achieved over a four line aggregation, using for that purpose a router with a four BRI module.

3 Technology Description

The implemented telemedicine infrastucture was based on the Medigraf® platform (see Figure 2). This system supports remote healthcare services, offering a collaborative work environment, videoconference and clinical data share.

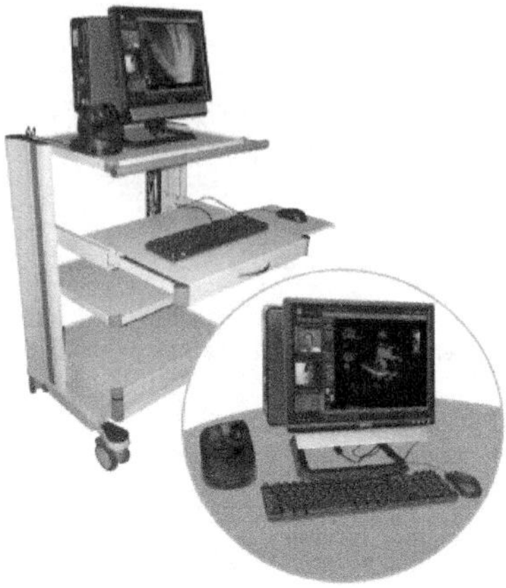

Fig. 2. The Medigraf® telemedicine workstation

The mobile telemedicine cart includes a computational base, a TFT LCD monitor, a pan-tilt-zoom camera, a microphone, speakers and a wireless headset.

The platform's software has a number of features which are shortly enumerated bellow:

- ✓ Multi-user access with login and password authentication;
- ✓ Encrypted communications over IP (Internet Protocol);
- ✓ Videoconference features;
- ✓ Collaborative work environment;
- ✓ Teleconsultation record management and storage;
- ✓ Interface to digital cameras, scanners and film digitizers;
- ✓ Real time transmission of clinical exams;
- ✓ Integrated DICOM image visualization and manipulation tool;
- ✓ Integration with Healthcare Information Systems and PACS;
- ✓ Web-based access, in intranet, for system and clinical data management;
- ✓ System usage reporting to monitor system utilization and access (lists of session's detailed information, statistics, etc);
- ✓ User-friendly interface.

By using this platform, healthcare professionals can remotely work together towards a common diagnosis, despite the physical distance that might be between them.

4 Methodology

A key aspect for the success of telemedicine projects, is the existence of a strong methodological approach that is being continuously refined as a result of the long time experience of the Pediatric Hospital of Coimbra in this area.

As a first step, previous to the usage of the technology, all the healthcare professionals and specialists that will be involved in the telemedicine project meet together at Pediatric Hospital of Coimbra and are exposed to the medical practices of the Pediatric Cardiology Service. Also the Portuguese physicians visit the involved African Hospitals, to take contact with the local health reality.

After that introductory stage, using the telemedicine infrastructure, the children are remotely observed in real-time and the heart pathologies diagnosed by the Portuguese physicians in close collaboration with the remote counterpart. During the Teleconsultation sessions the physicians share clinical data, echo-cardiograms and medical reports.

After the pathology identification, and in cases where local facilities are not available to solve the identified problem, such as is the case when a more specialized surgery is required, the local healthcare unit tries to transfer the children to other better equipped units.

5 Results

The Pediatric Hospital of Coimbra in Portugal holds a long experience in telemedicine. As a matter of historical data, Figure 3 displays the evolution in terms of the number of teleconsultations per year between this hospital and other Portuguese hospitals since 1998. Nowadays 8 Portuguese hospitals establish, in a regular basis, teleconsultations with the Pediatric Hospital of Coimbra.

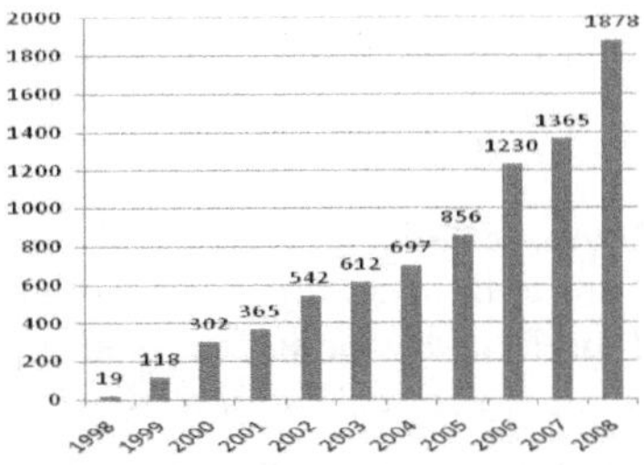

Fig. 3. Evolution of medical consultations using telemedicine in the Pediatric Hospital of Coimbra

This consolidated experience in Portugal, of more than 10 years, was crucial to launch in November of 2007 the first pilot of telemedicine with Angola (PEDITEL project). Since then, teleconsultations are running regularly between Pediatric Hospital of Coimbra and the two Angolan hospitals (Pediatric Hospital of Luanda and Hospital of Benguela). Figure 4 displays the number of teleconsultations performed in 2007 and 2008 between both Pediatric Hospitals.

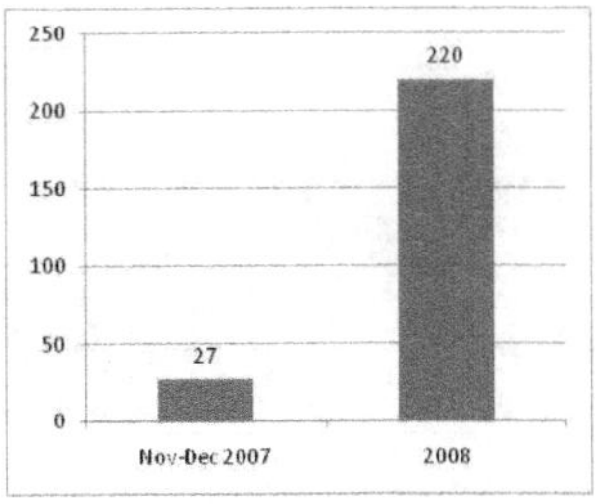

Fig. 4. Evolution of medical consultations using telemedicine in the scope of PEDITEL project

Up to now, more than 500 teleconsultations were done mainly in the area of Pediatric and Fetal Cardiology. There are also other clinical areas using the telemedicine system, namely Gastroenterology, Oncology and Infectology.

Figure 5 shows an Angolan physician being assisted by a Portuguese physician while an echocardiography to a children heart is being performed and transmitted in real time from Luanda to Coimbra using the telemedicine platform.

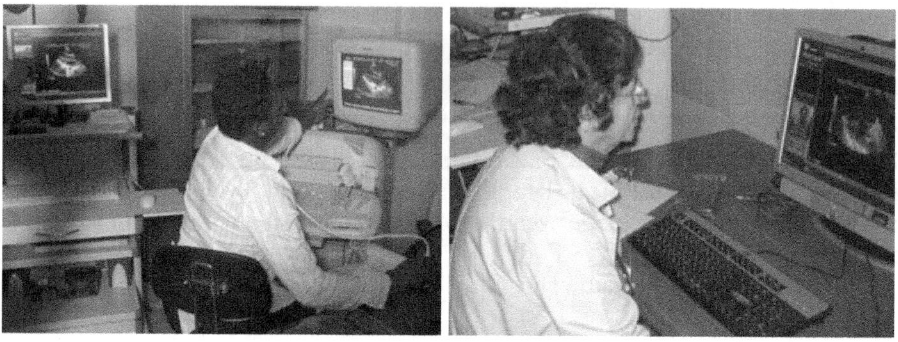

Fig. 5. Teleconsultation session between Pediatric Hospitals of Luanda (left) and Coimbra (right)

The physicians in Portugal are able to see in real-time the exam and identify the pathology. Moreover they are able to identify what should be done next, namely the steps the children should undertake, including their transfer to Portugal or other country for a possible surgery, given the fact that these facilities were not yet locally available in Angola. In situations where it was necessary to evacuate the patients to Coimbra by airplane, it became now possible to perform the medical diagnosis or confirm the diagnosis made earlier with a simple mouse click.

The installed technical infrastructure also has been applied, with high success, to the remote training of healthcare professionals (physicians, nurses, etc.). Since November of 2007, more than 5 tele-training sessions were performed between Pediatric Hospitals of Luanda and Coimbra, in areas like Pediatric Cardiology, Infectology and Pediatric Nursing.

Figure 6 shows pictures of the first tele-training session, in December 2007, with duration of two days and remotely attended by some tens of Angolan healthcare professionals.

Fig. 6. Tele-training session between Pediatric Hospitals of Coimbra and Luanda

Some sessions were performed from Coimbra to Luanda and other ones from Luanda to Coimbra. These tele-training sessions have contributed to the exchange of know-how and experience between these Portuguese and Angolan hospitals.

More recently, since May of 2009, Hospital Dr. Agostinho Neto (Cape Verde) started regular weekly teleconsultation sessions with Pediatric Hospital of Coimbra. Until now, more than fifty teleconsultation sessions were achieved between these two Hospitals, in the pediatric and fetal cardiology areas.

6 Conclusions and Final Remarks

African children in Luanda (Angola), Benguela (Angola) and Praia (Cape Verde) are already taking advantage of the telemedicine technology. Teleconsultations are occurring regularly between the involved hospitals. Given the results and experience already obtained, it can be concluded that the main benefits of the implemented telemedicine solution are related with the increase on the human resources efficiency, the decrease of the number of useless patient transfers to other hospitals and also the decrease on the number of unnecessary hospitalizations as well as the early identification to where the patients have to be transferred given the type of pathology.

Training, updating and knowledge share are other identified benefits. Moreover, it has also a pedagogical effect on the medical specialists from the central Hospital due to the fact that they will be exposed to some pathologies that no longer exist in developed countries and in that sense they also benefit from these experiences for their own proficiency development.

Cooperation is even taken further in terms of helping building surgery facilities and appropriate training to enable the local development of new medical capabilities and to locally expand the telemedicine.

The technology provided has been revealed as a user friendly mean to guarantee the local and independent operation whether by the physicians and/or network managers. A major impairment is typically the lack of telecommunication infrastructures at the remote areas, where interconnection circuits are mandatory. The cost of the circuits is of concern, mainly where there is a small offer, and the guaranteed 512 kbit/s bandwidth is not typically easy to get in many African countries.

The lack of specialized physicians is even a more severe problem once they are rare. This kind of technology is in fact the only one that allows for a faster widespread of specialized medical service in remote locations. From the social point of view the value of the service for the general population in the remote sites is priceless, and it constitutes a giant step forward in public health and general well being, with all the repercussions in the economic activities of those populations that came with it.

This type of network could also be expanded to other African countries with clear benefits to the local citizens and particularly to the youngest, due to the high children mortality rate in Africa. The development of an e-health network among the African countries could help in sharing experiences and allow for international cooperation with the foreign countries.

References

1. http://www.wisegeek.com/what-is-telemedicine.htm
2. Bukachi, Pakenham-Walsh: Information Technology for Health in Developing Countries. In: Chest 2007, vol. 132, pp. 1624–1630 (2007)
3. Geissbuhler, A., Bagayoko, C., Ly, O.: The RAFT network: 5 years of distance continuing medical education and teleconsultations over the Internet in French-speaking Africa. International Journal of Medical Informatics 76(5-6), 351–356
4. Geissbuhler, A., Ly, O., Lovis, C., L'Haire, J.-F.: Telemedicine in Western Africa: lessons learned from a pilot project in Mali, perspectives and recommendations. In: AMIA Annual Symposium Proceedings, pp. 249–253 (2003)

Implementing Mobile Phone Solutions for Health in Resource Constrained Areas: Understanding the Opportunities and Challenges

Tiwonge Davis Manda[1] and Jo Herstad[2]

[1] University of Malawi - Chancellor College, Mathematical Sciences Department, P.O Box 280, Zomba, Malawi
tiomanda@gmail.com

[2] University of Oslo, Department of Informatics, Gaustadalleen 23, P.O Box 1080, Blindern, N-0316 Oslo, Norway
jo.herstad@ifi.uio.no

Abstract. This paper presents results from a study on mobile phone use to connect two rural hospitals in Malawi with community health workers (CHWs), the hospitals work with. Mobile phone use at the hospitals has helped reduce the need for face-to-face communication to permit patient information exchange, meetings and appointments scheduling, as well as work coordination. On the other hand mobile phone use has proved paradoxical as it has introduced users to challenges, like recharging of phone batteries, they did not anticipate. The paper highlights use context-centric and solution based opportunities and challenges associated with mobile phone use in rural settings.

Keywords: mobile phones, use context, paradox, opportunities, challenges.

1 Introduction

Mobile phones have become an increasingly important information and communication technology. For example, 22 percent of Africa's population owned mobile phones at the end of 2006, compared to 3 percent with fixed telephone lines and 5 percent with Internet [18]. Furthermore, unlike personal computers and fixed line phones, mobile phones provide users with a high degree of independence, mobility and flexibility [2].

On the other hand, despite providing users with various benefits, mobile phone use also presents users with various unintended consequences (see [2] and [10]). Compared to static computing terminals, mobile phones are more susceptible to loss or damage, are resource-poor, have limited battery power, and their performance is highly variable due to gaps in network coverage (see [16] and [10]).

This paper is based on a study of mobile phone use to support health information exchange at two rural mission hospitals in Malawi. The hospitals, St. Gabriel's hospital and St. Martin's hospital, serve a total population of over 240 000 people, between them. At the hospitals mobile phones are currently being

A. Villafiorita, R. Saint-Paul, and A. Zorer (Eds.): AFRICOMM 2009, LNICST 38, pp. 95–104, 2010.

used to coordinate tasks and meetings, request urgent medical help, provide support to community health workers (CHWs), and relay patient updates between the hospitals and CHWs.

The paper addresses the following questions: How does the use context influence mobile phone use?; What opportunities and challenges are associated with the use of currently existing mobile phone solutions?

2 The Research Study

The study took a qualitative case study approach and was informed by the interpretive paradigm. Study data was mainly collected through semi-structured interviews. Additionally, document analyses, observations, and SMS log analyses were also used to gather additional data and cross-check data validity.

3 Literature Review

Some previous studies have shown that effectively working health information systems are necessary to ensure good health management (see [14] and [6]). For instance, providing timely and accurate data to managers in the health sector can enhance effective resource allocation and epidemic monitoring and control (see Lippeveld et al. [13] and [1]). However, the poor state of ICT infrastructure in developing countries limits successful ICT projects implementation [4]. This coupled with unreliable physical (e.g., roads and power supply) and communication infrastructure contributes to the underperformance of health management information systems in developing countries [11].

However, despite such challenges, mobile technologies can be used to enhance timely access to information at the point of care and enable health care professionals prescribe proper treatment [12]. It is critical, though to understand the context of operation when implementing mobile technology-based solutions. Their mobility and multiplicity of use contexts means multiple factors can positively or negatively influence their use [17]. Besides, understanding the local context of use is crucial in any technology's implementation process [19].

4 Conceptual Background

When implementing mobile phone solutions it is critical to realise that user interaction with such solutions is not independent of the use context's gravitational pull. According to Jarvenpaa and Lang [10] mobile phone use is influenced by, and influences, multiple situational factors that are technological, personal, organisational, and cultural in nature.

This paper builds on the argument that the use of mobile technologies gives rise to both intended and unintended consequences, and is therefore paradoxical. For example, *mobile technologies empower people and create new forms of enslavement* (empowerment/enslavement paradox). The use of mobile technologies *fulfils users' needs, but also creates needs* (fulfils needs/creates needs paradox). Furthermore, ownership of mobile phones can *create illusions of expectation* which if not met can lead to *user disillusionment* (illusion/disillusion paradox) (see [2] and [10]).

4.1 Information Infrastructure Theory

The paper also uses the concepts of *installed base* and *heterogeneity*, from the Information Infrastructure Theory (see [7] and [8]). The *installed base* concept emphasises that information infrastructures are not built from scratch, but rather from what is already in existence [7]. An *installed base* can, for example, comprise various integrated services and applications, their users and developers, as well as work practices that an infrastructure aims to support and embed [8]. *Heterogeneity* emphasises that information infrastructures are made up of a varied range of interdependent socio-technical components that are linked to conventions of practice, they influence and are influenced by [3].

5 The Case Study

The hospitals under study are currently using mobile phones to enhance communication between medical personnel and CHWs. This is being done in an environment where ICT infrastructure, with the exception mobile telephony networks, is poorly developed.

5.1 Mobile Phone Communication Setup and Management

The two hospitals have given out mobile phones to CHWs and some medical personnel to permit communication. Currently, St. Martin's hospital uses voice calls and St. Gabriel's hospital uses SMS to permit information exchange. Furthermore, St. Gabriel's hospital uses FrontlineSMS, an SMS management system, to log incoming and outgoing text messages.

Home Based Care (HBC) coordinators at the two hospitals link communication between CHWs and medical personnel. They monitor incoming and outgoing voice calls and text messages, and then re-route them to the appropriate addressees.

Besides providing a communication base the hospitals also set the tone for correct mobile phone use as illustrated in quote below:

> *"We were instructed to use this phone to call for an ambulance, when someone is sick." (CHW - St. Martin's hospital, 2008)*

5.2 Current Use of Mobile Phones

Currently mobile phones are, among other things, being used to reduce the need for face-to-face communication, to permit information exchange, between

CHWs and the hospitals. For example, CHWs are now able to remotely update the hospitals on their work and patients' medical status. Further to this, mobile phone use has also helped reduce the need for people to walk or cycle to distant villages, to announce arrangements for, or cancellations of, meetings and other appointments. The following quotes underscore these points:

> *"Previously we had problems submitting reports. Sometimes we had messages that needed to be communicated to the hospital on the same day. We, therefore, had to cycle to the hospital. Those who did not have bicycles would walk to the hospital." (CHW - St. Gabriel's hospital, 2009)*

> *"Currently, the hospital can communicate with us more easily. For example, I got the message for this meeting when I was out in the field gardening." (CHW - St. Gabriel's hospital, 2009)*

Furthermore, mobile phone use now permits medical personnel and CHWs to plan and share workload when organising patient follow-ups. For instance, voice calls or text messages are used to coordinate patient tracking and referrals, as indicated in the quote below:

> *"Please track patient A. The patient is not coming [to the hospital] for appointments." (HBC coordinator-St. Martin's hospital, 2008)*

More than this, mobile phones are also being used to remotely provide CHWs with expert medical advice on how to handle certain medical cases. In addition, at St. Gabriel's hospital, CHWs can now get reminders on how to administer various drugs via SMS. This is done by sending already fixed code-words, for various drugs, to the hospital's SMS management system.

5.3 Challenges Being Faced

Although mobile phone use has enhanced how the hospitals and CHWs interact and work, challenges exist. The challenges relate to *technological, organizational, personal, and cultural factors,* which together make up the use context.

Technological Factors

Existing technological challenges include lack of electricity connection in the homes of most CHWs, forcing them to walk long distance to recharge their phones; the existence of pockets with no cellular telephony network coverage and intermittent phone services; and the existence of poor road networks, which make it hard for people to access community phones or for the hospitals to quickly get to patients. The last two points are illustrated by the following statements:

> *"Another problem is the network especially for those who are coming from very far. You can text them an emergency message 'Please, can*

you come for a meeting tomorrow?' If there is no network they receive that message, maybe, two days later." (HBC coordinator- St. Gabriel's Hospital, 2008)

"Our villages are located in a remote area where roads are seasonal, so it becomes very, very difficult to travel from this village to the other... Transportation is one of the biggest problems." (HBC coordinator- St. Martin's hospital, 2008)

Organisational Factors

Existing organisational challenges include lack technical capacity to repair broken phones or further customize implemented mobile phone solutions, to meet changing needs; existence of weak monitoring and evaluation frameworks for measuring project impact and outcomes; and the cost of hiring an ambulance at St. Martin's hospital acts as a deterrent to community phones use, even though people can use the phones for free when calling for an ambulance. A CHW from St. Martin's hospital had this to say, in line with this:

"We told people in the villages that if they have a patient they can come to me so I call the hospital for help [an ambulance]. They don't come though. They are transported to the hospital by relatives who own cars, because the ambulance service is not free. People would not allow to be transported to the hospital using an ambulance when they can be transported there for free by their relatives. "(CHW - St. Martin's hospital, 2008).

Here the cost the cost of hiring an ambulance acts as a deterrent to an otherwise free service.

Personal Factors

At personal level, some community health workers at St. Gabriel's hospital have problems using free-form texting because they posses inadequate writing skills. At times, it is hard to decipher the meaning of text messages sent in by some CHWs. For example, in the message below a CHW wrote an entire message as one word:

"Mudwelekunokulimatendaenaofunikamutadwelakukaonamunenetsikulodwelazikomo"

Cultural Factors

Finally, at cultural level, Malawian traditional leaders are quite influential as regards what goes on in areas within their jurisdiction. For example, at St. Martin's hospital, chiefs were mainly influential in deciding to locate community phones at trading centres and close to main roads. This has made community phones less accessible to a considerable section of the target population.

6 Discussion

6.1 Influence of Use Context (Installed Base) on Mobile Phone Use

The mobile phone solutions under study here were introduced in an environment with already existing heterogeneous socio-technical systems. Among others, these included existing paper-based record management systems, mobile phone communication infrastructure, as well as organisational, personal, and cultural practices. Such pre-existing components provide the building blocks or installed base [8] on which the phone solutions, under review here, are built.

Organisational factors

These mobile phone solutions have been built on the hospitals' competencies and human as well as financial resources. For instance, the mobile phone solutions have been built on the hospitals' work and communication practices. Furthermore, the hospitals and their expectations help align users' ambitions when using their phones. On the other hand, as presented earlier, the cost of hiring an ambulance, at one of the hospitals, is deterring people from using community mobile phones to request ambulance services.

Cultural factors

Social and cultural characteristics can either enhance or limit ICT use and adoption, through shaping peoples attitudes and subjective norms [5]. For example since chiefs are quite influential in Malawi, involving them in project activities makes it easier to get their subjects on board. This, in turn, eases the rolling out of technologies within their communities. Building on already existing structures makes it possible for new innovations to leverage the installed base's strengths (see [7] and [8]).

On the other hand, relying on already existing components such as cultural norms does negatively influence mobile phone use, as various limitations inherent in the installed base are transferred to the mobile telephony projects. For example, the use of traditional authorities in determining where to locate CBO phones, has resulted in the phones being less accessible to some people.

Technological factors

Unlike stationary computers or fixed line phones, mobile technologies accord users more flexibility as regards when and where use occurs. Since mobile technologies can be carried along by a user they can be used in various places, as and when the user sees fit (see [20] and [9] and [10]). Due to such use flexibility, medical personnel and CHWs are able to communicate and coordinate activities, remotely. They are also able to communicate outside specified working hours.

On the other hand, technological limitations, like small screen sizes and tiny input keys make mobile phones unsuitable for other tasks. Even further, due to their mobility, mobile phones are subject to variations in performance because they rely on limited battery power and varying technical infrastructure to operate (see [16] and [10]). For example, recharging of phone batteries is quite problematic in rural settings like the hospitals where this study was conducted, as most people do not have electricity at home. Furthermore, pockets with no GSM network coverage within the hospitals' catchment areas, combined with intermittent mobile phone services, place limitations on *when and where* people can communicate.

Besides these factors, the conditions of other physical infrastructure like roads does enhance or limit the impact of phone use. For example, poor road conditions during the rainy season reduce the effectiveness with which phones can be used. As Hanseth and Lyytinen [8] put it, though heterogeneous, all components of an infrastructure are interdependent.

Personal factors

As has been previously put, the mobile phone solutions under study build on people's competencies to communicate. SMS-based communication, for example, relies on users' writing skills. Messages from users with low writing skills are potential error sources, as messages they write are hard to decipher. Moreover, it is difficult to maintain quality in free-form data entry, as inconsistent spelling and other mistakes are common (see Parikh et al. [15]).

6.2 Application-Centric Opportunities and Challenges: Paradoxes of Mobile Phone Use

Mobile phone use does not only end with achieving set user goals. Rather, it also gives rise to contradictory performances (see [2] and [10]).

The Empowerment/ Enslavement paradox

Opportunities: Empowerment
Mobile phone use at the two hospitals now allows users the freedom to communicate at unpredictable times and from unpredictable places. This is demonstrated by the ability of CHWs and medical personnel to communicate and collaborate remotely. Furthermore, at St. Gabriel's hospital, mobile phone use has empowered CHWs by enabling them to increase report submissions and cut down on the number of trips they make to the hospital. Mobile phone use reduces geographical and time barriers to communication, allowing users to communicate anytime, and from various unpredictable places [9]. Reducing the need for face-to-face meetings has enabled medical personnel and CHWs, at the hospitals where this study was conducted, to save on time.

Challenges: Enslavement
In as much as the use of phones empowers users, allowing users constant connectivity fuses work and spare time, as users are unable to separate and keep distance from work. This, then, means that users have less personal time, which can result in increased work pressure (see [9] and [10]). For example, for less experienced community health workers, giving patients anytime access to them, might lead to increased work pressure.

Fulfills Needs/Creates Needs paradox

Opportunities: Fulfilling Needs
As is evident from the case study, mobile phone use at the two hospitals has enabled CHWs to more constantly and quickly provide the hospitals with patient updates. This way the hospitals are better placed to provide better care to chronically ill clients. The use of mobile phones, at St. Gabriel's hospital, to remotely share and coordinate tasks also helps address the negative impacts of having few medical personnel who can conduct patient visitations. Furthermore, mobile phone use helps fulfil CHWs information needs on how to handle certain medical cases and administer medication.

Challenges: Creating Needs
Besides fulfilling various user needs, the use of mobile phones has exposed users to a range of problems. For example, users now have to worry about mastering the mobile phone solutions in use and any extensions that might be made. Furthermore, to be able to communicate, users have to worry about raising money for phone credit. Even further, the hospitals' HBC coordinators need to be constantly accessible due to the role they play in routing information between the hospitals and CHWs. This cannot always be achieved and introduces delays in information exchange, as the HBC coordinators also need to perform other duties.

The Illusion/Disillusion paradox

Opportunities or illusion?
The use of mobile phones brings with it so much promise. For example, owning a mobile phone gives the impression that one can take charge of situations and collaborate with colleagues and clients, *anytime and from anywhere* (see [10] and [9]). Mobile phone use also suggests improved information delivery, and expedited access to healthcare services since one can quickly request medical help. Additionally, the use of software such as FrontlineSMS that supports the redirection of text messages gives the impression that users can share information as and when they please.

Challenges: Illusions and disillusionment
Empirical evidence from the two hospitals under study shows that communication is only possible *sometimes and in some places*, due to incomplete network

coverage in some places. Furthermore, anytime communication requires that communication partners are available at the other end and willing to communicate [10]. To add on to this, at St. Gabriel's hospital, the FrontlineSMS system is switched of at night. This effectively means that text messages sent by CHWs at night remain undelivered until the next morning.

Apart from the factors above, FronlineSMS does not effectively support the notion of anytime anywhere communication. FrontlineSMS is a desktop system, making it harder for the system administrator to access and forward messages to other users, when out of office. Although FrontlineSMS supports text message forwarding to remote email accounts, this requires Internet access.

7 Conclusion

The implementation and successful use of mobile phone solutions in rural areas relies on factors such as the quality of existing infrastructure, cultural practices, and users' competencies. For example, SMS-based mobile phone solutions rely on users' writing competencies. Further to this, the paper has shown that the use of mobile phone solutions in rural settings faces challenges such as poor electricity connections and incomplete GSM network coverage. For example, due to incomplete GSM network coverage and intermittent mobile telephony services, at the hospitals where this study was conducted, it is not always possible for phone users to communicate *anytime and from anywhere*. Rather, they can only communicate *sometimes and in some places.*

In contrast to the above stated challenges, this paper has highlighted that even in areas where most ICT infrastructure is underdeveloped, mobile phone use can enhance communication between medical personnel and CHWs. The paper has also highlighted that mobile phone use has reduced the need for face-to-face communication to permit information exchange and work coordination. Furthermore, by using mobile phones to exchange patient updates with CHWs, and support the work of CHWs, the hospitals under study are now better placed to provide patients with urgent help, when need be.

Above all else, empirical evidence gathered in this study strongly suggests that users are willing to put in a lot of effort towards making mobile phone solutions work, if the solutions directly address their needs. Secondly, another key factor to successful mobile solutions sustainability is sustained and proactive isolation and minimization of user-technology conflict situations.

References

1. Abouzahr, C., Boerma, T.: Health information systems: The foundation of public health. Bulletin of the World Health Organisation 83, 578–583 (2005)
2. Arnold, M.: On the phenomenology of technology: The "Janus-faces" Of mobile phones. Information and Organization 13, 231–256 (2003)
3. Bowker, G.C.: The history of information infrastructures: The case of the international classification of diseases. Information Processing and Management 32, 49–61 (1999)

4. Dada, D.: The failure of e-government in developing countries: A literature review. Electronic Journal of Information Systems in Developing Countries 26, 1–10 (2006)
5. Erumban, A.A., Jong, S.B.D.: Cross-country differences in ICT adoption. A consequence of culture? Journal of World Business 41, 302–314 (2006)
6. Galimoto, M.S.: Integration of health information systems: Case study from Malawi. Department of Informatics. Oslo, University of Oslo (2007)
7. Hanseth, O.: The economics of standards. From control to drift - the dynamics of corporate information infrastructures. Oxford University Press, Oxford (2000)
8. Hanseth, O., Lyytinen, K.: Theorizing about the design of information infrastructures: Design kernel theories and principles. Case Western Reserve University, USA. Sprouts: Working Papers on Information Systems 4(12) (2005), `http://sprouts.aisnet.org/4-12` (accessed October 26, 2009)
9. Hurme, P.: Mobile communication and work practices in knowledge-based organizations. An Interdisciplinary Journal on Humans in ICT Environments 1, 101–108 (2005)
10. Jarvenpaa, S.L., Lang, K.R.: Managing the paradoxes of mobile technology. Information Systems Management 22, 7–23 (2005)
11. Kimaro, H.C., Nhampossa, J.L.: Analyzing the problem of unsustainable health information systems in less-developed economies: Case studies from Tanzania and Mozambique. Information Technology for Development 11, 273–298 (2005)
12. Kushchu, I., Kuscu, M.H.: From e-government to m-government: Facing the inevitable. In: European conference on e-Government (ECEG). Trinity College, Dublin, European conference on e-Government, pp. 253–260 (2003)
13. Lippeveld, T., Sauerborn, R., Bodart, C.: Design and implementation of health information systems, Geneva, World Health Organization (2000)
14. Lungo, J.H.: Data flows in health information systems: An action research study of reporting routine health delivery services and implementation of computer databases in health information systems. Department of Informatics. Oslo, University of Oslo (2003)
15. Parikh, T., Javid, P., Sasikumar, K., Gosh, K.: Mobile phones and paper documents: Evaluating a new approach for capturing microfinance data in rural India. In: Conference on Human Factors in Computing Systems, Montréal, Québec, Canada. Association for Computing Machinery, New York (2006)
16. Satyanarayanan, M.: Fundamental challenges of mobile computing. In: 15th ACM Symposium on Principles of Distributed Computing, Philadelphia, PA. Association for Computing Machinery, New York (1996)
17. Scheepers, R., Scheepers, H., Ngwenyama, O.K.: Contextual influences on user satisfaction with mobile computing: Findings from two healthcare organizations. The European Journal of Information Systems 15, 261–268 (2006)
18. United-Nations, The millennium development goals report, New York, United Nations (2008)
19. Walsham, G., Sahay, S.: Research on information systems in developing countries: Current landscape and future prospects. Information Technology for Development 12, 7–24 (2006)
20. Weilenmann, A.: Negotiating use: Making sense of mobile technology. Personal and Ubiquitous Computing 5, 137–145 (2001)

Application of Geographic Information System (GIS) in Drug Logistics Management Information System (LMIS) at District Level in Malawi: Opportunities and Challenges

Patrick Albert Chikumba

Department of Computing and Information Technology,
The Polytechnic, University of Malawi
Private Bag 303, Chichiri, Blantyre 3, Malawi
patrick_chikumba@yahoo.com

Abstract. District pharmacies in Malawi use a computerised IS to monitor the flow of products from a warehouse to health service delivery points and determine understocked or overstocked products at each health facility. Currently, all drug LMIS reports are in tabular forms. The GIS can help health and drug logistics officers to get additional spatial information, such as locations of health facilities and environmental factors, to the existing reports in the form of maps. This paper highlights some opportunities and challenges of applying the GIS in the drug LMIS, which basically involve technologies, organisation, and standards and data integration. It has been found that this idea is very good but it requires much effort, commitment and resources for successful implementation.

Keywords: Drug LMIS, Geographic Information System, GIS Implementation.

1 Introduction

In Malawi, there is a well established logistics management system which is the medical supply system of inventory management and recording and reporting for health commodities which ensures that all Malawians are able to receive products they need, and receive quality treatment when they visit a health facility. Health commodities move from major stores down to health facilities while the drug logistics information moves from the health facilities to the upper levels.

Currently, the district pharmacies use a computerised IS named the Supply Chain Manager which manages the supply chain information in the health commodity logistics management in the Ministry of Health (MoH). It helps drug logistics and health program managers determine which health facilities are understocked or overstocked among other information. But information on reports generated from this system is only in a tabular form. It is necessary for the drug logistics managers to have information about actual locations of health facilities and road networks for their day-to-day decision making. The GIS can be used in this case to provide such information.

The GIS can be applied in the drug LMIS with the aim to "enrich" the reporting of drug logistics information for the drug logistics and health managers at the district

A. Villafiorita, R. Saint-Paul, and A. Zorer (Eds.): AFRICOMM 2009, LNICST 38, pp. 105–115, 2010.

level. The managers can use the GIS to get additional information to the existing reports in the form of maps, which would show actual locations of health facilities, and other spatial information including the road network. Therefore, this paper discusses some opportunities and challenges that can exist when introducing GIS in the drug LMIS.

The GIS is one of the issues, which the government of Malawi is considering in its socio-economic policies. Even the MoH has a policy, which recommends the application of GIS in the health sector for instance, the GIS can be used in tracking and monitoring in terms of geographical variations in types and magnitude of problems and equity in distribution of health services across the country as well as service utilisation [7].

2 Literature Review and Theoretical Framework

The GIS does not in itself solve problems of development. It is necessary to consider also non-technical issues such as application environment, organisational issues, data exchange standards, legal issues and human resources.

2.1 Challenges in Implementation of GIS

Many literatures [1, 2, 3, 5, 6, 8, 10] have discussed about challenges, opportunities and strategies of developing and implementing the GIS in developing countries. Although implementation involves a considerable degree of technical issues, they are equaled or surpassed by organisational issues [10]. Croswell [1] argues that the technical side of system implementation and operation is considered "minor" as compared to organisational and institutional problems while standards and data integration are considered very important.

Data collection is one of the most time-consuming and expensive tasks of the GIS but very important because the effectiveness of the GIS depends on the degree of relevant data as input [6, 8]. It has been observed that it is more cost-effective to capture non-spatial data (attributes) separately from the spatial data. This is possible because it is relatively simple task that can be undertaken by lower-cost clerical staff and attributes can be entered directly, which does not require expensive hardware and software [5]. Alternatively, the spatial data can be obtained from external sources and one major decision that needs to be faced is whether to build or buy part or all of a database and the issue of data format. One of the biggest problems with the data obtained from external sources is that they can be encoded in many different formats because no single format is appropriate for all tasks and applications [5].

To fully realise the capability and benefits of the GIS technology, spatial data needs to be shared and systems must be designed and used by multiple organisations. According to Ginger [3] and Croswell [1], data exchange standards have key role to play for facilitating the integration of datasets from various distributed sources or organisations and lack of these required standards between organisations impedes data sharing.

Apart from availability of standardised data, the following are also required [1, 6, 10]: (a) the management (level of commitment, previous computing experiences, and style of leadership); (b) organisation (structure and operation, information flow, distribution of power, and cooperation among participants); (c) technology; and (d) user training including managers.

2.2 Drug LMIS as Installed Base for the GIS

Infrastructures are never developed from the scratch but develop through extending and improving the installed base. When a part of an infrastructure is changed, each new feature or component has to fit with the as-is infrastructure or installed base [4]. The installed base heavily influences how a new infrastructure can be designed i.e. an infrastructure inherits both strengths and limitations of the installed base upon which it builds.

The drug LMIS consists of work processes, systems, users, and procedures among other components. By considering how these components link or integrate, it is possible to identify which parts of the drug LMIS should be improved and extended in order to accommodate the GIS and also to determine which new components of the GIS should be introduced and being integrated with existing components.

3 Methodology

The framed experiment was the one used in this research with the focus on the following: (a) non-standard subject pool which consisted of pharmacy technicians, statisticians and pharmacy-in-charge; (b) experiences and information that the subject pool has with emphasis on the GIS and computer operations; (c) the GIS prototype treated as a new commodity to the drug logistics and health staff; and (d) demonstration of the GIS prototype to the subjects in their respective working places and subjects participated and provided feedback and comments.

The interviews were conducted with the aim of understanding working practices of the drug logistics staff and in the hierarchical manner starting from RMS in Blantyre, in the southern region of Malawi, down to its district pharmacies and district health offices (DHO) in Blantyre and Mulanje districts, and then two health centres in each of the two districts. This was supplemented by analysis of data collection forms and some reports from the Supply Chain Manager and direct observation on its data entry and reporting at Blantyre district pharmacy aiming on finding out how it handles drug logistics data.

Most data was collected through the evaluation of a GIS prototype whose spatial data was collected from the Department of Survey and Roads Authority. The GIS prototype was demonstrated to pharmacy technicians and statisticians from the Blantyre DHO and the pharmacist-in-charge from RMS in their respective working places. It was performed by applying the DECIDE framework [9] and drug logistics and health data of September 2008 was used. The demonstration focused mainly on (a) reporting and analysis of drug logistics information and (b) integration of spatial, drug logistics and health data. After the demonstration participants were interviewed for their feedback on the proposed GIS.

4 Findings

It has been found that the idea of introducing GIS in the drug LMIS is very good but it requires much effort, commitment and resources for successful implementation. Apart from the GIS being used only by the pharmacy technicians, other drug logistics and health staff were also interested in using it.

4.1 The Drug LMIS

The drug LMIS has the health facility, district, regional and national levels. There are a number of officers at each level responsible for managing drug logistics data and each officer has a role to play in LMIS. Data is collected at the health facility level and processed at the district level (district pharmacy) using different tools in order to produce required logistics information for decision making. The responsible level reports within a fixed period of time to the upper level which is supposed to send feedback to the lower level and concerned stakeholders.

For the drug LMIS to function properly, it requires people, data, work processes, tools, equipment, policies, procedures and transport systems among others. The relationships and interactions of these elements and systems form an installed base which the proposed GIS can be built on. Work processes in the drug LMIS include data collection, processing, analysis, and reporting which governed by the standard procedures and policies.

Supply Chain Manager
Ministry of Health
Blantyre District

Stock Imbalances
Report Period: September, 2008
All Facility Type
Health Centre

Run Date:
Run Time: 04:19 PM
Page: 1 of 1

Facility	Product	Closing Balance	AMC	Months of Stock	Quantity Required	Status
Chimembe HC	Sulphadoxine 500mg/pyrimetherine	0	4,000	0.0	12,000	Stocked Out
Bangwe HC	Sulphadoxine 500mg/pyrimetherine	3,000	4,333	0.7	9,999	Below Minimum
Dziwe HC	Sulphadoxine 500mg/pyrimetherine	5,000	6,000	0.8	13,000	Below Minimum
Makata HC	Sulphadoxine 500mg/pyrimetherine	1,000	4,000	0.3	11,000	Below Minimum
Soche HC	Sulphadoxine 500mg/pyrimetherine	2,000	4,000	0.5	10,000	Below Minimum
Zingwangwa HC	Sulphadoxine 500mg/pyrimetherine	13,000	15,667	0.6	34,001	Below Minimum
Chavala HC	Sulphadoxine 500mg/pyrimetherine	21,000	1,667	12.6	-15,999	Overstocked
Limbe HC	Sulphadoxine 500mg/pyrimetherine	11,000	3,333	3.3	-1,001	Overstocked
Lirangwe HC	Sulphadoxine 500mg/pyrimetherine	19,000	2,000	9.5	-13,000	Overstocked
Lundu HC	Sulphadoxine 500mg/pyrimetherine	17,000	2,667	6.4	-8,999	Overstocked
Madziabango HC	Sulphadoxine 500mg/pyrimetherine	10,000	333	30.0	-9,001	Overstocked
Mpemba HC	Sulphadoxine 500mg/pyrimetherine	21,000	1,333	15.8	-17,001	Overstocked
South Lunzu HC	Sulphadoxine 500mg/pyrimetherine	12,000	2,333	5.1	-5,001	Overstocked

Fig. 1. Drug LMIS Report from Supply Chain Manager

The drug logistics data is collected at the health facility by health staff using LMIS forms at the end of every month. Then the LMIS forms are sent to the district pharmacy for processing and analysis using the computerized system, Supply Chain Manager. This system generates different type of reports in tabular form (see Fig. 1) that are sent as hard copies to RMS, district health management team (DHMT), and some stakeholders on monthly basis and on request. The district pharmacy uses these reports to respond to all emergency orders from the health facilities and redistribution of some health commodities from overstocked to understocked health facilities. RMS uses the same information to decide on the monthly distribution of health commodities to the health facilities.

In the drug LMIS, there exist various work processes, users (pharmacists and health staff), tools and equipment (forms, computers and printers), policies and procedures which are linked together in one way or another. The interconnections among these elements or components form the installed base which the GIS as a new system can be built on. It is important to identify which work processes, users` responsibilities, tools and equipment, and procedures among others of the drug LMIS should be extended and/or improved in order to accommodate the GIS.

4.2 The Proposed GIS

For the proposed GIS to be implemented in the drug LMIS, it requires expansions and additions in some areas such as work processes, technologies, people and organisational issues. Work processes in the proposed GIS are data collection, data management, data integration, data processing and analysis, and reporting. Although data collection, reporting, processing and analysis are available in the drug LMIS, they need some extensions in order to be supported in the proposed GIS.

The data collection in the drug LMIS involves only drug logistics data which is part of non-spatial data of the proposed GIS. It is essential to collect spatial data of district administrative boundaries, health facilities, pharmacies and road networks as required in the drug LMIS. Currently, MoH does not collect any spatial data which means that it needs to outsource the services from other organizations, such as the Survey Department, that are already experienced in the spatial data collection. The required non-spatial data includes drug logistics data, health data, and attributes of districts, health facilities, pharmacies and roads. The collection of drug logistics and health data is already in place due to existence of drug LMIS and HIS and what is required is to integrate them with spatial data.

A new work process to be added is the data management which will involve updating of spatial data and attributes. For instance, spatial data used in the GIS prototype has required some updates of districts, health facilities, and road networks. The attributes of health facilities need to be modified now and again.

The data integration is also a new work process to be introduced in the proposed GIS (see Fig. 2). Health managers require drug logistics data and on other hand drug logistics managers require health data on their decision making. Therefore, the proposed GIS can be used as an integration tool to link the logistics and health data together through a common geographical reference system of the health facility.

The specific processing and analysis of drug logistics and health data are performed by their respective systems. For example, the drug LMIS processes and analyses the logistics data which result in the stock status (adequately stocked, overstocked or understocked) of each health commodity and this information can now be integrated with the spatial data and displayed on the map. In some cases it is required to process and analyse data after integration with spatial data for better presentation on the map.

The proposed GIS requires producing reports for use but since the reports contain graphics it is important to consider the best way of production. The map display can be a main method of reporting because it will allow the pharmacy technicians to interact with the map. Printing can be taken as second option when a hard copy is required and it requires high quality colour printing.

Since the GIS should be used at the district pharmacies to support the reporting of drug logistics information, it means that the main user of this system is the pharmacy technician. The pharmacy technician can be assisted by health staff especially in data collection, integration and management. Health facilities are in the management of health staff so it is very important to have them involved. Since it will be the first time to use the GIS at the district pharmacy, it is necessary to train the pharmacy technicians and health staff on how to use the GIS software, tools and equipment. It is also wise to outsource the expertise in human resource or even tools and equipment in the spatial data collection as Mennecke & Crossland [6] point out that data acquisition can be difficult and costly issue in the implementation of the GIS.

The Supply Chain Manager which is used at the district pharmacy only produces reports in tabular form as pointed earlier. For instance, the stock imbalances report (see Fig. 1) of the shows that out of twenty-one catchments health facilities in Blantyre, six were understocked and seven were overstocked but it was not known what happened to other eight health facilities, whether they were adequately stocked, or did not give SP to patients (no consumption), or did not report.

Comparing Fig. 1 with Fig. 3, it was found that the spatial reporting can be a supplement to the original report which shows actual location of the health facility and how far it is from the district pharmacy. It shows that in September 2008, three health facilities did not report any data on SP and only five were adequately stocked. For example in Fig. 1, Chimembe health centre was out of stock of SP and required emergency supply and at the same time three health centres were much overstocked. Therefore, the map (see Fig. 3) would help drug logistics managers to decide which health facilities SP drugs could be transferred from, based on distance and accessibility between understocked and overstocked health facilities.

It is summarised that the existing installed base (drug LMIS) could accommodate the GIS by doing the following: (a) extending the work processes to accommodate the spatial data collection, integration and management; (b) extending policies, procedures and standards for governing the work processes. (c) extending the use of the computers to run the GIS software which would provide tools for integrating the drug logistics, health and spatial data and acquisition of new hardware and software; (d) extending the staff's responsibilities and tasks to those who are involved in spatial data collection, integration and management and in using the GIS software and hardware tools; (e) establishing links between the MoH and other organisations, that deal with spatial data, for sharing of spatial data and outsourcing of expertise (human resource) and tools; and (f) improving the printing quality for colour graphics output of maps. However, there exist challenges and opportunities of fulfilling these suggested activities in order to apply the GIS in the drug LMIS.

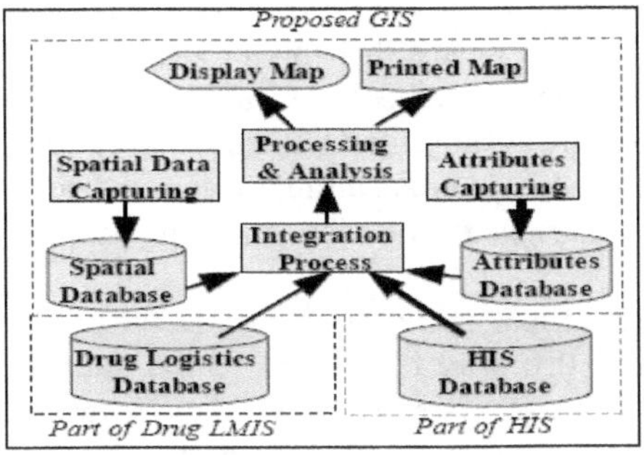

Fig. 2. Integrating Databases of GIS, Drug LMIS & HIS

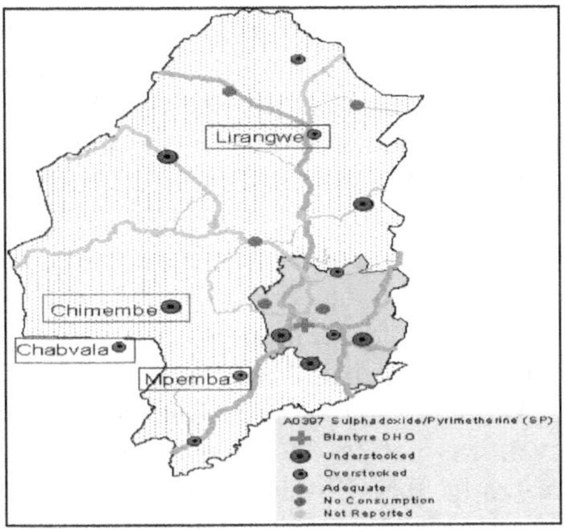

Fig. 3. Generated Map from GIS prototype for Stock Status Reporting

5 Opportunities and Challenges

5.1 Opportunities and Challenges on Standards and Data Integration

The new work processes (spatial data collection, integration and management) are the most time-consuming and expensive GIS tasks but very important because effectiveness of the GIS depends on the degree of relevant data as input. For DHO to successfully implement the GIS in the drug LMIS, it is important to consider carefully data standards and integration particularly between the GIS, drug LMIS and HIS.

The DHO can minimise the cost of building spatial database by outsourcing the expertise from some organisations that are experienced in spatial data collection because this exercise requires well-skilled people, very powerful equipment and also time. The available GPS at DHO can only be used to collect new spatial data for updating the spatial database. It is not necessary to spend a lot of resources to acquire those equipment for and train user on spatial data collection, which is already being done by some organisations. Most of organisations that deal with spatial datasets are from the Government of Malawi which MoH is part of and hence it is very easy to establish relationships between the ministry and those government departments for spatial data sharing.

The main challenge is the data standards for data sharing. Since the spatial data will be outsourced, it is needed for DHO, in particular, and MoH, in general, to determine data standards for easy sharing of spatial data with other organisations because the data from external sources can be encoded in many different formats. For instance, although the Department of Surveys is the national mapping agency and mandated by the legislation to carry out base mapping and control mapping in Malawi, it has its own spatial data standards and formats that may not be relevant to the MoH to use in its GIS as observed in the GIS experiment where the spatial data required some updates before using in the GIS prototype.

DHO requires collecting non-spatial data including drug logistics and health data which should be done separately from the spatial data because it is relatively simple task that can be undertaken by lower-cost staff and attributes can be entered directly which does not require expensive hardware and software. The health and drug logistics data are collected by health and logistics staff using simple materials and equipment such as forms and ordinary computers which means that this process does not require well-skilled person and complicated techniques and equipment as compared to the collection of the spatial data. There are already systems that handle the drug logistics and health data and what the DHO will need is to concentrate on the updates of attributes of health facilities, road networks, pharmacies, districts and other required features in the spatial database.

Although, it is taken to be very cheap to collect non-spatial data at the district level, it is not easy to integrate the data from HIS, drug LMIS and spatial database. Currently, the HIS and drug LMIS are independent systems having their respective policies, standards and procedures. A common identifier is required in all three databases for easy integration and management. It is necessary to determine standards for the common identifier, in this case the health facility and naming of different features such as health facilities, pharmacies and districts. For example, all databases should use the common codes and names for health facilities and pharmacies. If this is to be implemented, it means that the DHO will have a lot of work to modify all codes and names of health facilities and pharmacies in the drug LMIS and HIS to match with those in the spatial database.

If there is a certain change, it will be necessary to update all three databases in order to maintain data consistency and this update will be in hands of two offices the pharmacy technician (for drug logistics database) and statistician (for health database) which require a good coordination. Since both the drug LMIS and HIS will not only be used to feed the GIS, it is important to make sure that the databases have complete data for other services.

Another challenge is a definition of data collection points in the drug LMIS and HIS as experienced in the GIS experiment. In the HIS data is collected from the catchments health facilities while in the drug LMIS data is collected from any health facility which gets health commodities from either RMS or the district pharmacy. It means that to integrate data from the two systems, it is required to define common collection points for both drug logistics and health data. Otherwise data from some health facilities, that are not data collection points in either one of the systems, will be difficult to integrate.

5.2 Opportunities and Challenges on Organisation

The management plays a key role in achieving the GIS adoption and some factors that influence the effective use of the GIS technology are a level of commitment, previous computing experiences, and style of leadership. There are several things that have already been done at DHO. The Government of Malawi in general and MoH in particular have shown some level of commitment on the use of GIS in Malawi in terms of policies and support. The government has come with the GIS policy among socio-economic policies which results in various governmental departments, such as Roads Authority and Survey Department, to be now involved in the GIS. MoH also plays its role to promote the GIS usage by, for example, documenting the GIS policy in the health sector and purchasing GPS for DHO for the spatial data collection.

MoH has already implemented some IS at the district level and experiences that it got during those implementations can be applied to determine ways of implementing the GIS at DHO. The mentioned IS include the district health information system (DHIS) and Supply Chain Manager for the drug LMIS. But it has been observed that these systems are different from the GIS and therefore, the implementation of GIS can be somehow different from those of the two systems. The GIS requires some specific work processes that are not needed in the DHIS and Supply Chain Manager such as spatial data collection, data integration and sharing which require specialised training and equipment, and special consideration in terms of a cooperation among participants from different levels of the drug LMIS and relationship between the Ministry of Health and other institutions including governmental departments.

Currently, at DHO, there are some health and logistics staff members, especially pharmacy technicians and statisticians, who are capable of using different information technologies. They use computer systems in their daily work and have necessary computing skills, knowledge and experiences. It is possible that they can be given further training on the GIS technologies especially on data collection, spatial database management, and use of the GIS software applications.

The issue is now how the user training will be conducted. Some studies have shown that the most programs are normally carried out as part of software training packages and not integrated with the work practices that surround the use of the GIS technology [3]. For the GIS to be implemented successfully, MoH should analyse user needs especially work practices of the pharmacy technicians and health staff in order to incorporate them in the training. It is also necessary to educate the health and drug logistics managers on the benefits of the GIS technologies so that they can provide their necessary support to the implementation of GIS in the drug LMIS. It seems that it will need a lot of effort and commitment in order to conduct the suggested user training because according to the research findings there have been some plans before for user training on the GIS but not yet fulfilled. Since the acquisition of GPS in over four years ago, there has been no any type of training on how to use the technology.

The introduction of GIS will also result on extra responsibilities and tasks to the pharmacy technicians and statisticians who are already overloaded with work due to the lack of human resource in MoH. Alternatively, MoH can outsource the GIS expertise from institutions or organisations such as the Survey Department, particularly on the spatial data collection and building its necessary database. The drug logistics and health staff can only be trained on data management (updates) and use of the GIS software tools.

The effective use of GIS at the district level requires also cooperation among participants from all levels as emphasised by Croswell [1] that the cooperation among participants at different levels of organisations, especially government, is a key to a successful integrated information systems, such as the GIS. The research findings have shown that the cooperation exists in the drug LMIS between staff from all levels, from health facilities up to the national level. MoH in general and CMS in particular need to maintain that cooperation when introducing the GIS. It is very important to extend this cooperation to health staff and other departments in order to, for example, share the spatial data and expertise. Apart from the pharmacy technicians, it has been observed that the GIS would be used by the health staff and logistics staff at the district. All parties should agree on common goals and individual benefits should also be identified.

A sufficient structure, at DHO, is needed for communication channels as well as for resolution of power and control conflicts that can exist due to the introduction of the GIS. Mennecke & Crossland [6] argue that the GIS is likely to have significant impacts on the structure and operation of the organisation. It seems that this can also happen at DHO through changing of the information flow which definitely affects the distribution of power. Through extending responsibilities and tasks of the pharmacy technicians and statisticians, they will get additional power and will definitely share the power with other individuals due to collaborations and interactions. The new operations such as spatial data collection, sharing and integration will also be added to the existing ones. Even Sieber [10] found out that the implementation of the GIS tends to alter the organisation substantively because it is expensive and complex and usually it frequently crosses departmental/subunit lines and alters power relations as the control of information changes.

5.3 Opportunities and Challenges on Technology

The practical work of GIS always involves some aspects of technology which focuses on the computer hardware, software and technical support. The availability of computers, printers, GPS, software systems and users having computing capabilities can be considered as an opportunity in the sense that they will provide technical support to the application of GIS in the drug LMIS. The same computers, that are used in the drug LMIS at DHO, can also be used to run the GIS software. Apart from computers, each DHO has got a GPS which is very important in the spatial data collection due to its advantage of less time-consuming, less expensive, and simpler to use than other techniques such as ground survey, scanning and digitising. The users of these computers, particularly pharmacy technicians, have computing skills and experiences which will provide basic technological background for easy knowledge transfer of the GIS technology when it comes the time of user training.

Availability of the technologies discussed above is not enough to have the full operational GIS in the drug LMIS. Every GIS requires the software tools which include interface, database, analytical and communication tools among others. Currently, DHO has no any GIS software which is in use. It is needed to purchase or acquire necessary GIS software that will provide all required functionalities. For instance, in the United Kingdom well-known GIS products include ArcInfo and ArcView from ESRI, GeoMedia from Intergraph, MapInfo Professional from MapInfo Corp, and GeoConcept from GeoConcept [2]. This shows that there are several GIS software technologies from various vendors or organisations with specific purposes and therefore, it is important for MoH to do a certain software analysis to recommend the most suitable GIS software that will be used in all DHO.

6 Conclusion

The GIS can be taken as the information reporting tool in the drug LMIS in which the GIS will integrate drug logistics data with the spatial data and display on the map. It can be concluded that successful implementation of the GIS in the drug LMIS at the district level in the Ministry of Health will depend on: (a) good evaluation of needs of the pharmacy technicians; (b) long-term commitment to the proposed GIS project of the various program managers in the Ministry of Health especially those dealing with the drug logistics; (c) sufficient allocation of resources and adequate staffing; (d) timely and sufficient training to the pharmacy technicians; and (e) good establishment of cooperation of participants and with other organizations and departments for easy sharing of the spatial data and expertise.

References

1. Croswell, P.: Obstacles to GIS Implementation and Guidelines to Increase the Opportunities for Success. Journal of the Urban and Regional Information Systems Association 3(1), 43–56 (1991)
2. Forster, M.: Review of the use of Geographical Information Systems in the Marketing and Planning of Logistics Services. Christian Salvesen Logistics Research Paper no. 3 (2000)
3. Ginger, L.J.: Introducing Geographical Information Systems for Health Care in Developing Countries: Challenges and Approaches, A case study from Mozambique. Master Thesis, University of Oslo (2005)
4. Hanseth, O., Lyytinen, K.: Theorizing about the design of Information Infrastructures: design kernel theories and principles. Working paper at University of Oslo, Department of Informatics (2005)
5. Longley, P., Goodchild, M., Maguire, D., Rhind, D.: Geographic Information Systems and Science, 2nd edn. John Wiley & Sons, Ltd., Chichester (2005)
6. Mennecke, B.E., Crossland, M.D.: Geographic Information Systems: Applications and Research Opportunities for Information Systems Researchers. In: Proceedings of the 1996 Hawaii International Conference on System Sciences, HICSS-29 (1996)
7. Ministry of Health and Population: Health Information System: National Policy and Strategy. Malawi Government (2003)
8. Saugene, Z.B.: Challenges, Opportunities and Strategies for Using Geographic Information Systems for Public Health Management - An Action Research Study from Mozambique. Master Thesis, University of Oslo (2005)
9. Sharp, H., Preece, J., Rogers, Y.: Interaction Design: Beyond Human Computer Interaction, 2nd edn. John Wiley & Sons, Chichester (2007)
10. Sieber, R.E.: GIS implementation in the grassroots. Journal of the Urban and Regional Information Systems Association 12(1), 15–29 (2000)

Converged Infrastructure for Emerging Regions - A Research Agenda

Nicolas Chevrollier, Juha Zidbeck, Ntsibane Ntlatlapa, Burak Simsek, and Achim Marikar

nicolas.chevrollier@tno.nl, juha.zidbeck@vtt.fi, nntlatlapa@csir.co.za, {burak.simsek,achim.marikar}@fokus.fraunhofer.de

Abstract. In remote parts of Africa, the lack of energy supply, of wired infrastructure, of trained personnel and the limitation in OPEX and CAPEX impose stringent requirements on the network building blocks that support the communication infrastructure. Consequently, in this promising but untapped market, the research aims at designing and implementing energy-efficient, robust, reliable and affordable wide heterogeneous wireless mesh networks to connect geographically very large areas in a challenged environment. This paper proposes a solution that is aimed at enhancing the usability of Internet services in the harsh target environment and especially how the end-users experience the reliability of these services.

Keywords: AMC, beamforming antennas, cross-layer, network monitoring, cognitive self-configuration and self-management, converged infrastructure;

1 Motivation and Concept

The internet penetration in Africa is still extremely low (2-3%) and even less in rural areas. In year 2007, there were only two million fixed broadband subscribers in whole Africa where the population is about 1 billion. Especially, the penetration in Sub-Saharan region is very low due to the lack of required telecommunication infrastructure and low gross domestic product per capita. Nevertheless, the trend in the growth of Internet services is very promising especially when looking at the growth rate of other ICT services.

When compared with the internet usage, mobile telephony has found a substantial acceptance in those regions (See Figure 1). There are currently more than 250M subscribers in all over Africa, and this number has increased exponentially over the years.

One of the most influential reasons behind this discrepancy between the penetration of mobile services and internet services lies in the fact that internet costs are extremely high in Africa due to the lack of terrestrial networks and high usage of satellite based Internet services.

Even if a price reduction about 25% is considered from year 2006 to 2007, it is clear that mobile telephony costs nearly one fourth of internet services. Additionally, the Internet services in Africa were in year 2006 over twice more expensive than in Europe. When the gross domestic product (GDP) per capita is taken into account [1],

A. Villafiorita, R. Saint-Paul, and A. Zorer (Eds.): AFRICOMM 2009, LNICST 38, pp. 116–125, 2010.

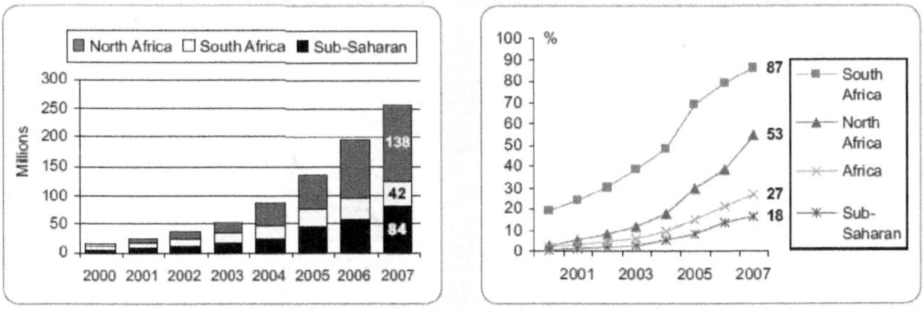

Source: ITU World Telecommunication/ICT Indicators Database.

Fig. 1. Mobile Services in Africa 2001 – 2007 [ITU]

the Internet service costs are twenty to thirty times more expensive in Africa than in Europe. Therefore, it is clear that Internet services are currently beyond the reach of most people in Africa.

One of the key reasons is the lack of reliable infrastructure especially in rural areas. This paper proposes a solution that is aimed at enhancing the usability of Internet services in the harsh target environment and especially how the end-users experience the reliability of these services. The main objective is to design and implement energy-efficient, robust, reliable and affordable wide are heterogeneous wireless mesh networks to connect geographically very large areas in a resource challenged environment.

2 Vision and Challenges

What is the future in terms of communication infrastructure in rural Africa? There are over 400 000 localities on the continent, of which 99 percent are villages, up to two-thirds of the people live in rural areas. In these areas, less than four percent have a fixed line telephone connection and while mobile communications have made huge inroads in providing connectivity to villages, about half of African villages were not covered by a mobile signal in 2006. In few cases where Internet access is available, it is provided via expensive satellite connection. There are isolated cases where satellite Internet access is extended to surrounding villages via the deployment of infrastructure-less networks such as mesh networks (mesh islands). Examples of such exist in South Africa and in Zambia [7].

In our vision, the mesh islands will be interconnected and these interconnected heterogeneous (WiFi, Wimax, satellite, cellular networks) mesh networks will provide the (wireless) terrestrial connectivity covering very large areas as depicted in Figure 2. Consequently, communication infrastructure in emerging regions (Africa and parts of Europe) will be based on heterogeneous wireless mesh networks to connect geographically very large areas in an extremely harsh environment.

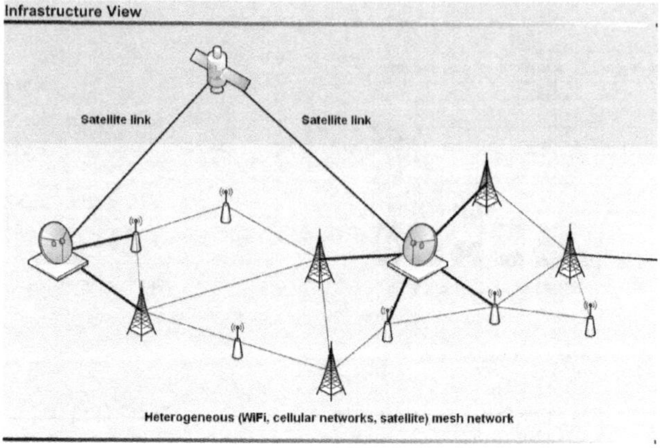

Fig. 2. Converged Infrastructure for Emerging Regions

Imposed by the characteristics of the harsh environment, the following key challenges of the envisaged wireless mesh network should be solved:

1. **Lack of reliable energy supply;** R&D challenges include:
   a. energy-efficient equipment and communication technologies (including communication protocols)
   b. energy supply based on solar power and radio/network/management technologies/approaches to handle limitations and variations in power supply
2. **Lack of wired infrastructures;** Hence, the wireless mesh will be very large in terms of distance and in terms of hops. This requires routing protocols that can handle and adapt to the specifics of multi-hop wireless, particularly considering a lot of lousy hops, unreliable nodes and limited bandwidth. R&D challenges include:
   a. development of radio infrastructures for large area wireless multi-hop multi-technology connectivity
   b. development of routing protocols that support such a mesh-topology infrastructure efficiently
3. **Lack of well-trained service-personnel;** leading to the requirements of self-configuration, self-management and self-healing equipments and protocols. R&D challenges include:
   a. development and deployment of self-managed and self-healing equipment
   b. development of adaptive radio technologies for these environments
   c. determination of network dynamics and development of respective network management and service provisioning mechanisms
4. **Limitations to OPEX and CAPEX due to limited financial capabilities of target customers** (in order to ensure a business case for sustainable network deployment); Equipment needs to be low-cost enabling local operators to provide affordable services to some or all potential users. In Africa, the monthly mobile prepaid average tariff basket was US$ 12 in 2007.

3 Example

In order to highlight the confronted environment that imposes the same requirements on the infrastructure that needs to be developed, a view of a typical rural African settlement is shown in the picture below. As can be seen from the type of vegetation, multi-path effects and scattering are relatively low. Also, the relative position between houses shows that, typically, there are at least one or a couple of low buildings in the immediate vicinity of each other. The distances between sets of buildings are in the order of few hundred meters to a few kilometres. The height of the buildings on the one hand simplifies propagation but on the other hand does not provide any sufficiently tall infrastructure for efficient broadcasting. The solutions for a typical city environment may not be appropriate for the environment depicted here.

Fig. 3. Typical landscapes of rural South Africa

One of the challenges in rural Africa is the lack of reliable power supply. Typical solutions for these are to power devices with batteries that are sometimes recharged by solar energy. Under these conditions, some of the communicating nodes are bound to run out of power and fail, i.e. become unavailable for routing any messages. In a traditional network with fixed hierarchy, this scenario would mean unavailability of communication for all the nodes which rely on the failed node for relaying their messages. The mesh network topology provides greater flexibility and permits self-healing of the communication infrastructures, taking advantage of alternative routing. Under this scenario, the low-cost solutions such as the one depicted in Figure 4 will not work as it requires manual intervention to change its direction. Appropriate solutions need to have the ability to change direction automatically. Smart antenna systems have the ability to change the direction of the beam on demand permitting a quick switch-over to an alternative route. Another challenge is scarcity and often absence of skilled personnel. The ability of a system to perform as much of the setting up, re-configuration, balancing etc. seamlessly and automatically is critical for making communications available and sustainable in the short to medium term.

Fig. 4. Installation of a DIY kit for wireless communications, provided by the Meraka Institute of CSIR

Figure 4 shows installation of a do-it-yourself WiFi based communication kit deployed by the Meraka Institute of CSIR in the recent past. The antenna used is made of a metallic coffee can. This antenna, just as most of traditionally used antennas are fixed to the wall, does not have any degree of control. Thus, the link cannot be changed without manual intervention.

4 Relevant Work

Project	Missing elements
CARMEN	Carrier-grade mesh networks (CARMEN) looks at mesh networks through the view of a telco operator [2]. In particular, it is assumed that the network is very well planned, energy is not an issue and neither are costs. Well-trained engineers are always at hand relieving several of the typical constraints in wireless mesh networks. In Africa, we do not have the comfortable fully controlled environment of CARMEN, neither the requirements to provide 24/7 carrier-grade service.
WIDENS	A validation of Mobile Ad-hoc Network (MANET) deployment for emergency case was done in FP6 project WIreless DEployable Network System (WIDENS) [3]. To cope with the situation in Africa, a complement of WIDENS' scope is needed by considering other radio broadband links and also by demonstrating how ad-hoc networking helps to offer interaction with other wireless connections such as satellite and existing narrowband system.
Self-NET	Self- management of cognitive future internet elements (Self-NET) focuses on self-management of network nodes and subnets based on a cognitive feedback-control cycle. While Self-NET assumes a rather stable infrastructure, where network dynamics typically arise from changing traffic patterns, due to the situation in Africa environmental impacts on

Project	Missing elements
	network capability, stability and performance need to be considered. In addition, Self-NET (like most other projects) assumes an abundance of energy and transmission capacity to be available for internal network management. Additionally, there is no mesh relevant scope of Self-NET.
SOCRATES	Self-Optimisation and self-ConfiguRATion in wirelEss networks (SOCRATES) [4] project aims at the development of self-organisation methods to enhance the operations of wireless access networks by integrating network planning, configuration and optimisation into a single, mostly automated process requiring minimal manual intervention. While SOCRATES focuses mainly on cellular networks, concepts developed in this project could be reused for a converged infrastructure in emerging regions.
N4C	Networking for Communications Challenged Communities (N4C) [5] project is looking at ways to extend Internet access to remote regions that do not have reliable and affordable network access today. N4C focuses particularly on Delay Tolerant Networks while for a base providing an always-available infrastructure is needed.
FMFI	First Mile First Inch (FMFI) [6] is a project that was conceptualised by the Wireless Africa team at Meraka Institute of the CSIR with the aim to identify and develop models and technology in order to overcome the problem of access to communication and information services in low-density (rural) areas. In FMFI, no architecture for converged infrastructure is provided.

5 Objectives and Outcome

Based on the challenges mentioned in the previous section, the clear objective is to design and implement energy-efficient, robust, reliable and affordable wide area heterogeneous wireless mesh networks to connect geographically very large areas in a challenged environment. This general objective is translated into a number of more specific objectives organized along the following themes:

- The development of novel Adaptive Modulation and Coding (AMC) and smart beamforming antennas to adapt radio transmission to the availability of energy
- The development of a network monitoring based on self-configuration/self-management techniques deployed in a large multi-radio meshed converged infrastructure to cope with the lack of human resources and wired infrastructure
- The design of a cross-layer architecture to support message forwarding mechanisms in order to optimize power consumption and content delivery

After being equipped with the proposed ICT solutions, the envisioned system will have a key role in enhancing the usability of internet services in the harsh target environment and especially how the end-users experience the reliability of these services. The objectives are further detailed out in the remainder of this section.

5.1 To Develop a Novel Adaptive Modulation and Coding Scheme to Optimize Energy Consumption

The concept of adaptive modulation and coding (AMC) is to change the Modulation and Coding Schemes (MCS) dynamically with the changing channel condition to increase the overall spectral efficiency. The AMC schemes will be used to adapt radio transmission to environmental changes (weather conditions), transmission requirements (amount of data) and availability of energy.

5.2 To Develop Smart Beamforming Antennas to Optimize Energy Consumption

Smart beamforming antennas will be used to develop an inexpensive energy- and spectrum- efficient smart antenna system for replacing the commonly used omni-directional antennas. This antenna system will be able to focus the radiated/received electromagnetic energy in a specified direction. This lowers energy consumption, improves spectrum re-use, channel capacity and/or increases the communication range.

In order to access all available neighbouring nodes, this antenna requires steering the beam over the 360 degrees in the horizontal plane. An *intelligence engine* will provide the ability to identify the sources of interference, to form radiation patterns shaped to be insensitive in the direction of interference found and to tune the transmitter's output power to a minimum necessary level. A cross-layer mechanism will permit switching between routes/directions according to the commands from the medium access control (MAC) or networking layers.

The ability to command the shape of antenna's radiation pattern and position the beam in the desired direction, as well as information derived from the link and channel measurements, will be used to simplify set-up and maintenance of the network, contributing to self-configuration and self-management.

5.3 To Design a Cross-Layer Architecture to Support Message Forwarding Mechanisms in Order to Optimize Power Consumption and Content Delivery

Such a cross layering approach will require an interface among different network layers enabling the exchange of the information and respective software modules that are able to receive and interpret this information. IEEE 802.21 is a nice example for a cross layer protocol enabling the cooperation between MAC layer and the upper layers. With an approach similar to IEEE 802.21, we will define primitives between neighbouring layers enabling both central and distributed information exchange including energy specific information, end-user characteristics and network properties such as the vulnerability of TCP connections to SATCOM links, which is widely the case in rural areas.

5.4 To Develop a Network Monitoring System and Cognitive Self-configuration and Self-management Mechanisms to Cope with the Unreliability of the Environment of Emerging Regions

Intelligent network monitoring will be used to reduce the amount of information required for assessing performance and experienced QoS of coexisting wireless systems. The problem is that the most important indicators e.g. end-to-end delay or end-to-end jitter cannot be obtained reliably and collected data from networks contain a high degree of irrelevant data, which gets needlessly processed.

Another objective is to alleviate problems originated from lack of technical personnel, unreliable power supply and abnormal traffic load situations in a multi-system environment by enhancing self-configuration and self-management capabilities of network nodes. These capabilities are also essential to ensure sufficient quality of service for end-users and maximal utilisation of scarce radio resources. Providing intelligent and agile self-configuration and self-management support for coexisting networks is essential.

5.5 To Create a Converged Infrastructure to Improve the Use of Different Available Wireless Network Access Means

A converged infrastructure for emerging regions includes a mesh-network where several compositions of multiple transmission technologies will be available routing traffic from source to destination alternatively. An example might be a choice between interconnected WiFi-stations, longer-range Flash-OFDM and meshed satellite links (both composed and alternatively). For this purpose, the most appropriate technologies (e.g. IEEE 802, 3GPP, LTE, Flash-OFDM, DVB...) suitable for the envisioned regions of Africa and Europe and the expected demand for connectivity within those regions will be determined.

In order to provide generic support for service continuity across these networks, it is necessary to describe and propagate service requirements and to set and request link-layer functions and capabilities (also for alternative paths of concatenated links). Hence, a media independent interface for the management of the determined technologies will be prepared. Different than IEEE 802.21, this interface will have the main focus on building and managing *heterogeneous mesh networks*. Hence, the studies will concentrate either on a new protocol dedicated to media independent mesh technologies or on an amendment to the existing IEEE 802.21 extending its functionalities for mesh networks.

6 First Steps towards a Solution

LinkNet Zambia [7] has been developing a WiFi based mesh solution for rural Macha, which is located in the Southern Province of Zambia. Because of the lacking fibre connection to the core network, Internet is provided through two satellite gateways based on C-Band (128Kbps downlink / 256Kbps uplink) and Ku-Band (512/256Kbps). Due to high costs of satellite connection, the available bandwidth is distributed throughout other facilities in need of internet connection via a mesh network. For the efficient functioning of the mesh network, different components such as monitoring and load balancing modules are already implemented.

However, the very dynamic structure of the region requires that the available bandwidth is further propagated to nearby campuses, such as the Ubuntu Campus that is about 3km away from Macha centre. Considering the low available bandwidth, frequent power downs and the harsh climate of the area, this is a challenging task; but on the other hand a one-time opportunity for a proof of concept. Therefore, Fraunhofer FOKUS is now developing a WiFi based solution based on the concepts of this study. The solution should build the basis for a more developed architecture ensuring reliable and efficient network utilization both in Macha Centre and Ubuntu Campus in the long term.

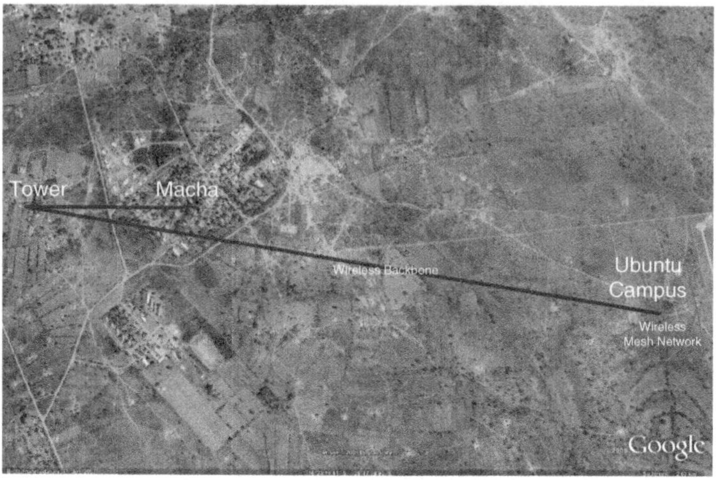

Fig. 5. Connecting Ubuntu Campus and distribute Internet access wireless

Currently, for the long distance connection of Macha with Ubuntu Campus low cost WiFi devices are deployed. Within Ubuntu Campus the connection is supplied through a mesh network. The target is to further improve this testbed so as to enhance the functionalities of these devices by smart software and inexpensive additional hardware. In order to increase the available bandwidth and the stability of the network, advanced routing protocols and autonomic configuration of the physical layer are developed. Transmission power, modulation type and used frequencies can be adapted automatically if a physical layer with cognitive skills is used. In addition to different antenna types like omnidirectional, yagi and parabolic, also smart antennas adapting to the current situation, e.g., by changing directions in case of node failure, will be used.

7 Conclusions

To provide a communication architecture for emerging regions, there is a need for a holistic approach to tackle a number of challenges described in this paper (lack of reliable energy supply, lack of wired infrastructures, lack of well-trained service-personnel, limitations to OPEX and CAPEX due to limited financial capabilities of target customers). The robust and reliable resulting infrastructure will be supported by a wide range of technologies (heterogeneous WiFi, Wimax, satellite, cellular networks) providing vital services to the population. The envisioned social impact is tremendous in line with the potential market share gain. Finally, to enable this research roadmap to come true, a strong cooperation is needed between research institutes from emerging and developed regions supported by a favourable policy environment.

References

1. African Telecommunication/ICT Indicators 2008: at a crossroads, ITU, 8th edn. (2008)
2. CARMEN, Seventh Framework Program, CARrier grade MEsh Networks, http://www.ict-carmen.eu/
3. WIDENS, Sixth Framework Program, http://www.comlab.hut.fi/projects/WIDENS/
4. SOCRATES, Seventh Framework Program, http://www.fp7-socrates.eu
5. N4C, Seventh Framework Program, http://www.n4c.eu/
6. First Mile First Inch project, http://www.fmfi.org.za
7. LinkNet Zambia, http://link.net.zm/

Author Index

GPSR Compliance

The European Union's (EU) General Product Safety Regulation (GPSR) is a set of rules that requires consumer products to be safe and our obligations to ensure this.

If you have any concerns about our products, you can contact us on ProductSafety@springernature.com

In case Publisher is established outside the EU, the EU authorized representative is:

Springer Nature Customer Service Center GmbH
Europaplatz 3
69115 Heidelberg, Germany

Batch number: 10854054

Printed by Printforce, the Netherlands